THE BOMBARD STORY

L'Hérétique at Ciudadela, Minorca

Dr Alain Bombard

THE
BOMBARD
STORY

TRANSLATED BY
BRIAN CONNELL

READERS UNION
ANDRE DEUTSCH
LONDON 1955

This Readers Union edition was produced in 1955 for sale to its members only by Readers Union Ltd at 38 William IV Street, Charing Cross, London, and at Letchworth Garden City, Hertfordshire. Full details of RU may be obtained from either of these addresses. This edition has been reset in 11 on 12 pt Joanna type, printed and bound at The Aldine Press, Letchworth, Hertfordshire. The book was first published in France under the title 'Naufragé Volontaire' and in England by André Deutsch Ltd.

CONTENTS

FOREWORD

EARLY one morning in the spring of 1951 I was asleep in the residents' quarters of the hospital at Boulogne-sur-mer when the telephone rang:

'Is that the house surgeon?'

'What is it?'

'A ship has been wrecked on the Carnot mole.'

'I'll come at once.'

Grumbling to myself, with no inkling of how serious the accident was, I dressed quickly and hurried down to the casualty ward. No patients had yet arrived. I asked the night porter what had happened and he told me that a trawler, the Notre-Dame-de-Peyragues, from the little port of Equihem, had missed her course in the mist and had hit the outer end of the Carnot mole. This outer breakwater of the harbour is very dangerous in bad weather, but easy to scale at other times as there are ladders every twenty yards along its face. The weather was cold, but the sea was calm and I was not unduly anxious.

Then came the sound of the siren of the fire engine. The double doors were thrust open and I took a couple of steps towards the entrance, full of my own importance. . . . I shall never forget the terrible spectacle of those forty-three men piled one on top of the other, like dislocated puppets, their feet bare, and each still wearing a lifebelt. In spite of all our efforts we failed to revive a single one. An error of navigation lasting a few moments had caused forty-three deaths and orphaned seventy-eight children.

I think it was at that moment that the full measure of tragedy conjured up by the word 'shipwreck' was brought home to me. The seed was sown for what developed into the expedition of L'Hérétique. Shipwreck became for me the very expression of human misery, a synonym for despair, hunger and thirst. Boulogne alone lost between a hundred and a hundred and fifty fishermen every year and I discovered that throughout the world in time of peace more than two hundred thousand men – and women – suffered the same fate. More than a quarter of them, having survived disaster and reached the boats, died afterwards in mortal agony.

For some time I had made a study of the resistance of the human organism to privations, and had convinced myself that it was possible for an individual to survive beyond the limits normally assigned by physiological science. I had paid particular attention to the case histories of political deportees, prisoners and undernourished populations. But, with my background as a doctor, for whom the teachings of science remain a dead letter unless they can find practical application, my theoretical studies only seemed to lead to the question: 'What use can be made of this knowledge?'

The problem of shipwrecked survivors found its natural place in such a study. It had one special characteristic: the external conditions contributing to this particular form of human misery were not, as in the case of prisoners and the like, due to the malice of man, about which nothing can be done; nor were they due, like the famines of the Far East, to natural disasters such as drought, against which one can do little. They depended on a natural element, dangerous without doubt, but nevertheless rich enough in the necessities of life to ensure survival until the arrival of aid or the sighting of land.

There are nearly two hundred times as many living

organisms in a cubic foot of water as in the same amount of earth.

Although the sea represents a constant danger to the shipwrecked man, it is not malicious and is certainly not sterile. The conquest of fear and the search for sustenance should not present insurmountable difficulties. That was my basic premise as far as the environment was concerned. I had also become convinced that in their studies of the capacity of the human organism to survive in such circumstances, the physiologists had not made enough of will-power and its influence on physical reactions. It is only necessary to recall the fasts of Gandhi, the Polar expeditions of Scott and Amundsen and the voyage of Captain Bligh, who lived for forty days on eight days' provisions, sustained by his hate for his mutinous crew. It is not a question of survival being possible in certain defined conditions, but rather, to use the formula so dear to mathematicians, 'other things being equal' (thus allowing latitude for the effect of the will, by which I understand courage and determination to live), survival is certain if specific physical conditions are met.

I turned back to my statistics again: could nothing be done to save those fifty thousand people who die every year in lifeboats, and if so what? At first, the classic stories of shipwreck which I then began to study seemed to rule out the possibility of any additional factor turning the scale.

The frigate La Méduse was lost on 2nd July 1816, on a sandbank about a hundred miles off the African coast. One hundred and forty-nine of the survivors – passengers, soldiers and a few officers – had to trust themselves to a hastily constructed raft towed by the ship's boats. The tow broke in circumstances which have never been explained and the raft was abandoned to the fury of the Atlantic. There were six barrels of wine and two of fresh water on board, but the raft was not sighted again until twelve days later. By then there were only fifteen survivors, ten of whom died shortly after rescue.

On 15th April 1912, the liner Titanic hit an iceberg in the North Atlantic and sank in a few hours. When the first relief ships arrived, three hours after the liner had disappeared, a number of people had either died or gone mad in the lifeboats. Significantly, no child over the age of ten was included among those who had paid for their terror by madness and for their madness by death. The children were still at the age of reason.

These examples confirmed for me the overwhelming importance of morale. Statistics show that ninety per cent of the survivors of shipwreck die within three days, yet it takes longer than that to perish of hunger and thirst. When his ship goes down a man's whole universe goes with it. Because he no longer has a deck under his feet his courage and reason abandon him. Even if he reaches a lifeboat he is not necessarily safe. He sits, slumped, contemplating his misery, and can hardly be said to be alive. Helpless in the night, chilled by sea and wind, terrified by the solitude, by noise and by silence, he takes less than three days to surrender his life.

How many castaways through the ages have become stiff and sudden corpses, killed, not by the sea, not by hunger or thirst, but by their own terror? I became convinced that most of them had died long before the physical and physiological conditions had of themselves become fatal. How was one to combat despair, a far more ruthless and efficient killer than any physical factor?

PART ONE

THE PLAN
TAKES SHAPE

CHAPTER I

SPONSOR

〜 〜 〜 〜 〜 〜 〜 〜 〜 〜 〜

TOWARDS the end of September 1951, one of my rivals in that year's attempts to swim the English Channel, Jean van Hemsbergen, suggested we should go sailing together. He was trying out a new type of dinghy. As soon as my turn of duty at the hospital was ended, I joined him on the beach, where I found him about to launch an inflatable rubber dinghy. The floats were shaped like a horseshoe, the open end closed by a wooden stern-board. It was the forerunner, on a smaller scale, of L'Hérétique, the boat in which I made the voyage described in this book. We set off at about four o'clock in the afternoon to test the outboard motor.

It was a lovely day. 'What about making for Folke-stone?' Jean suggested. It seemed a splendid idea, so we set off north-north-west, steering for the South Foreland, and picking up the flashes of its lighthouse as night fell. The wind rose and the sea became quite rough, but the Hitch Hiker, as the dinghy was called, behaved admirably and we entered Folkestone harbour about eleven o'clock. I had no passport, but the British authorities did not raise any difficulties.

The weather quickly deteriorated, and soon it was blowing half a gale out of the North Sea. In spite of the confidence we had in the dinghy we thought it better to wait for the wind to die down. We did venture outside the harbour once, but it seemed madness to continue, so we turned back. The gale showed no signs of abating and I realized that the hospital would be getting worried. I had sent off a telegram to tell them where I was, but I still felt I should get back for duty as my spell as house physician did not end until 1st October. Ignoring advice, we decided to risk it and set off at nine o'clock the next morning. We almost gave up at the harbour bar, but it was, after all, a lifeboat we were trying out, and survivors do not choose the weather in which to be shipwrecked. Nine times out of ten when they have to take to the boats it is in the middle of a storm.

We met the sea head on and expected at any moment to have the motor swamped. But everything went well, Hitch Hiker rode the waves magnificently and on we went across a channel quite free of its normal traffic. After several narrow escapes we reached the beach at Wissant at about six o'clock in the evening. The dinghy had proved its worth.

We were met on arrival by a man who was to become for some time my patron and backer. He was a Dutchman, well known as an expert in salvage and life-saving equipment, a big fellow, about six feet tall and weighing all of twenty-five stone. He had a fine open face, great powers of persuasion and a frank nature. Or so I thought at the time.

We took to each other at once and in the course of our conversations over the next few days he put forward the idea of establishing a grant which would enable me to work out in detail in a laboratory my half-formed theories on the possibilities of survival at sea. I was to establish scientifically the minimum necessary intake of food and drink, and then we would all three set out on a sea voyage to prove that we had found the means of saving future castaways from despair. I was also to map out a possible course, while our sponsor would see to the provision of the necessary equipment. We decided that I ought to start on my studies at the Museum of Oceanography in Monaco and that our expedition would take place about the end of the year.

Fate then took a hand. I began my experiments earlier than I expected by becoming a castaway, as people usually do, against my will. Before leaving for Monaco, van Hemsbergen and I were due to make a quick trip to England for the wedding of one of our friends. On Wednesday, 3rd October, while we were trying out a new motor in the dinghy off Wissant, it broke down about three miles north-north-west of Cap Gris-Nez, and we started to drift. We had only been making a short trial and we had on board neither sail nor any other means of propulsion. The wind was from the north-north-east and drove us along for two days and three nights with no hope of approaching land. Although the coast was out of sight we knew we must be drifting roughly parallel to it and that after the mouth of the Somme it turned west again, so we were not unduly worried. With any luck we should end up between St Valéry and Dieppe. Finally, on the Friday, at about nine o'clock in the morning, we sighted a trawler, the Notre-Dame du Clergé, and tried to head towards it by using the dinghy's waterproof as a makeshift sail. Modest resources are often the way out of great difficulties, a lesson which was not lost on me. For two days van Hemsbergen had drunk nothing at all. I on the other hand had taken a little sea-water to quench my thirst, knowing that in such quantities I ran no risk. The only food we had was a pound of butter, which one of us had brought on board by pure chance – and butter is not exactly the thing to quench one's thirst.

The trawler picked us up and van Hemsbergen buried his head in a bucket of fresh water. Convinced that I too must be thirsty, I did the same, but at the second swallow I stopped. I found that I was not really thirsty. Thanks to my régime of sea-water I had not become dehydrated and in fact needed no drink. It was a striking example of the way in which preconceived ideas can influence the organism to the point of inducing an apparent need where none really exists.

Three days later I read in one of the local newspapers: 'Alain Bombard picked up half-dead from hunger near St Valéry.' People were already beginning to dramatize my activities, in spite of the fact that when we had hurried to catch a plane at Le Touquet in order not to miss the wedding in England, we had obviously been in quite good form. Nevertheless the authorities were on our trail. I was soon involved in the first act of a scenario which provided, at the most unexpected moments, a number of vexatious episodes, both during my preparations and the actual voyage. I have called it, with apologies to Courteline, the Comic Interlude.

The first scene took place in an office full of desks, each piled high with papers. Behind one of them a naval captain sat pontificating. I was given a chair in front of him, like a naughty schoolboy who refuses to acknowledge his guilt.

'Do you realize that you have committed an offence in leaving territorial waters without a navigation permit?'

'But a certain latitude is granted to small boats.'

'That is so, but only those described as beach craft. And it is not stated anywhere that they may leave territorial waters.'

'Is it stated that they may not?'

'There is nothing in the regulations about that.'

'Well, then?'

But my interrogator put an end to the interview by saying: 'In any case it is quite impossible to overlook your continual infringements.'

'Are you not going to take into account the fact that I was only a passenger and that the owner was on board?'

'I am under no obligation to answer you: I will let you know my decision in due course.'

We parted on bad terms, but, as at the end of each of these episodes, there was some compensation. In the waiting room I met another naval captain, a real seaman this time, named Maupéou, who greeted me warmly and said: 'Well done, old chap.'

CHAPTER II

PURPOSE

∽ ∽ ∽ ∽ ∽ ∽ ∽ ∽ ∽ ∽ ∽

I ARRIVED in Monaco on 19th October and went to pay my respects at the Museum of Oceanography, with a request that I might be included among the research workers to whom they allowed the use of a laboratory. I was received by the deputy director, M. Belloc, whose interest in my experiments never wavered and who has remained my good friend. I was at once given all the facilities I needed, and wasted no time in getting down to work.

It will be easier for readers to follow the events described in this book, if they bear with me, first, in an account of what was known, and what was thought to be known, on the subject of saving life at sea when I started my detailed studies. The expedition itself, first through part of the Mediterranean and then across the Atlantic, was merely an attempt to prove in practice what I was already sure of in theory, after my laboratory work on the subject. Unless I state now what I was setting out to prove, the incidents of the voyage would lose their point. It is essential to give certain facts concerning nutrition, the reactions of the human organism, the contents of the sea and the characteristics of certain fish. All this had to be studied before I set off, and I hope I am right in thinking that a short account of it will be more useful here than if it were tucked away in an appendix.

Shipwrecks fall into two categories, those that occur on

the coast and those on the high seas. Of the two hundred thousand human beings who die every year as the result of accidents at sea, just over half lose their lives in coastal wrecks. Assistance is usually at hand for the survivors, through the devoted labours of the lifeboat institutions in each country.

On the high seas the situation is different. Here about fifty thousand unfortunates die each year, more or less at the moment their ship goes down. That leaves another fifty thousand who might be saved. They, in their turn, fall into two categories.

There are two sorts of ship. First, the big liners and naval vessels in permanent radio contact with land the whole time they are at sea; if one of them founders, everyone knows almost exactly where the disaster has happened and other ships hurry to the rescue. We have seen the example of the Titanic. What the survivors need is simply a 'morale injection', to enable them to regard rescue as a certainty. The problem of a prolonged fight for survival hardly presents itself.

Then come the other types of vessel, cargo boats, tramps, deep-sea trawlers and fishing boats in general. Normally their radio contact with land is limited to a fixed 'rendezvous' every six, twelve, or sometimes only every twenty-four hours. Between each signal they may cover a considerable distance. If something happens to them, their exact position is difficult to determine and the lot of the survivors is correspondingly grim. These are the men and women who were always uppermost in my thoughts and whom my experiment was designed to assist. To my dismay I discovered that relatively little is done for them. If their ship goes down they are considered as lost. Only in the most favourable circumstances does a search last for as long as ten days and even then very little hope is entertained of sighting them. After ten days it has become usual to abandon the search on the grounds that there is no longer any hope of finding them alive. The explanation given is that neither human being nor equipment can be expected to hold out longer than that. My object was to give these unfortunates a better chance of reaching land. Several thousand widows less per year seemed to me an objective fully justifying the risk of one life.

           ∽   ∽   ∽   ∽   ∽   ∽   ∽   ∽   ∽

My research work came under five headings. I looked up every possible reference on:

1 The history of previous shipwrecks and the lessons to be learnt from them.
2 The case histories of survivors.
3 Fish and their chemical composition.
4 The various methods of catching fish.
5 The study of favourable winds and currents.

At the same time I tried out on myself in the laboratory various experiments with abnormal food, while van Hemsbergen, who had come to join me, concentrated chiefly on the study of the best type of craft for our purpose. The whole ground had to be carefully covered. Over a period of six months the day's work varied from the chemical analysis of sea-water to a minute study of the various types of plankton, together with laborious analyses of the chemical composition of different species of fish. I took as my basic premise the fact that although a lifeboat or life-raft may in theory be equipped with every conceivable type of apparatus, much of it might have been washed overboard by the time it was required.

           ∽   ∽   ∽   ∽   ∽   ∽   ∽   ∽   ∽

Almost on the first day I managed to turn up a basic document in the latest issue of the Bulletin des Amis du Musée Océanographique. It was a reprint of a report made to the Paris Academy of Sciences on 17th December 1888, by Prince Albert I of Monaco, himself the founder of the museum.

'I consider it useful to communicate to the Academy', the Prince had written, 'an account of certain striking investigations of ocean fauna carried out in conjunction with other scientific studies over the last four years by L'Hirondelle. Experiments during 1888 proved conclusively that an abundance of sea fauna could be caught during the night hours.

'A fine silk net with an opening of about eight feet, towed on the surface for about half an hour, always brought in a considerable quantity of fish (Scopelidae) and about four and a half inches of edible organic matter.

'A simple landing-net of the same material, about twenty inches wide, plunged at night into one of the shoals of jelly fish often encountered in the Atlantic, would bring up about one cubic inch of the small crustaceans (Hyperia Latreillei) which are usually to be found in their company.

'In the Sargasso Sea there is a whole family of marine life to be found hidden amongst the fronds of the floating seaweed in this area. It is made up of both crustaceans and fish, in even greater quantities than those just mentioned, but they are often not perceived at first glance because of their similarity in colouring to the weeds themselves.

'During the months of July and August 1888, L'Hirondelle made a study of the occurrence of tunny fish up to a distance of six hundred leagues to the west and south-west of Europe: two lines with artificial bait caught fifty-three tunny fish with a total weight of one thousand pounds.

'Submerged wrecks and flotsam, sufficiently old to have attracted barnacles, are always accompanied by quite sizeable fish. Six such objects were inspected in July and September, and it was possible to catch twenty-eight sea perch with a combined weight of three hundred and thirty-four pounds. During this and previous seasons there was no difficulty in catching almost any amount of these fish (three hundred and thirty-one pounds on one day alone) without seeming to diminish the numbers round the wreck in any way.'

This report made it quite clear that shipwrecked survivors in the North Atlantic, and probably any other ocean in the temperate regions, could escape death by starvation if they had the following equipment:

1 One or several nets of straining cloth, between three and six feet in diameter, on about sixty feet of line, in order to pick up the smaller sea fauna.

2 Several fishing lines about one hundred and fifty feet in length, ending in three casts of brass wire attached to a large hook, with some sort of artificial bait, for tunny fish.

3 A small spear or harpoon with which to catch the sea perch which are attracted to flotsam, and a few brightly polished hooks, which these fish will often take without any bait.

4 A large harpoon with which to catch any of the larger fish which collect round wreckage.

The Prince ended his report by stating firmly that with this knowledge and equipment it should be possible for the survivors of a shipwreck to maintain life until help arrived.

◇   ◇   ◇   ◇   ◇   ◇   ◇   ◇   ◇

My next problem was to show that the sea provides not

only food but a sufficient and balanced diet. The ocean supplies three things: sea-water, fish and plankton. This latter group is made up of the millions of microscopic creatures which are to be found in any sample of fresh or salt water. They fall into two main groups: the zooplankton (i.e. the planktonic animals and fish roe) and the phytoplankton, or planktonic plants, composed mainly of algae or microscopic seaweed. Plankton is of enormous biological importance, as all animal life in the sea is ultimately dependent on it for existence. It is, moreover, the principal food of whales, the largest existing mammals.

The average composition of sea-water (taken from Jean Rouch's *Traité d'Océanographie Physique*) is as follows:

COMPOSITION OF SEA-WATER

The amounts of salts dissolved in one gallon
of average sea-water

$NaCl$	45·0 ounces	
$MgCl_2$	5·6	,,
$MgSO_4$	3·3	,,
$CaSO_4$	2·1	,,
KCl	1·0	,,
$CaCO_3$	0·2	,,

The chemical analysis of such fish as I was likely to catch during my voyage gives the following figures (table, p. 14) for the three principal constituents, water, fat and protein (taken from Creac'h, *Les Protides Liquides du Poisson*). With plankton, the composition is much more variable and much less known, and I spent most of my time in concentrating on this in an attempt to track down some of the elements of nutrition which I knew were still lacking. I was in the position of a man who has been given a limited amount of material and is told, 'With that you must build a house'. I set to work.

PRINCIPAL CONSTITUENTS OF FISH
Percentages by weight

FISH	WATER %	PROTEINS %	FATS %
Ray	76·80 – 82·20	18·20 – 24·20	0·10 – 1·60
Basking shark	68·00	15·20	16·00
Dolphin	77·00 – 78·89	17·25 – 19·00	1·00 – 3·31
Ray's bream	78·90	18·42	0·34
Sardine	78·34	16·30 – 21·00	2·00 – 12·00
Anchovy	76·19	21·92	1·11
Bonito	67·50 – 69·17	18·52 – 24·00	7·00 – 12·46
Bass	77·00 – 79·94	18·53 – 19·96	0·84 – 2·50
Mullet	75·60	19·50	3·90
Mackerel	68·84 – 74·27	17·59 – 23·10	5·14 – 8·36
Tunny	58·50	27·00	13·00
Fish roe	48·80 – 78·31	11·50 – 45·90	1·16 – 16·20

The principal problem was water. Everyone knows that drinking is more important than eating. Ten days without water result inevitably in death, but a man can survive for thirty days without food. Where was I to get my fresh water from? I soon reached the conclusion that the fish themselves were going to provide me with all I needed. The previous table shows that a fish is made up of between fifty and eighty per cent by weight of water. Moreover, it is fresh water, and this was the liquid on which I intended to rely against thirst.

Have you ever had to eat fish which some careless cook has forgotten to season? It is completely insipid. I proved by analysis that the flesh of fish is greatly inferior in sodium chloride (common salt) to that of mammals – with one or two exceptions to which I shall refer again when considering the subject of proteins. If only I could extract the liquid from the flesh I would get all the water I needed from between six and seven pounds of fish a day. The problem was to extract it, which was not a laboratory question.

But what was to happen if I caught no fish? This is often the case during the three or four days after a ship sinks, and that is the critical period. If there is nothing to drink, the body's water content will decline steadily until death by dehydration occurs on about the tenth day.

Any supply of fresh water or fresh liquid which becomes available at a late stage of this process, needs to exceed the day's basic requirement, if it is to restore the body to a normal condition. The survivor has to 'catch up' on his body's water content, and not just satisfy his day-to-day needs. The essential thing, therefore, is to maintain the body's water content at its proper level during those first few days before fish can be caught.The only solution is to drink sea-water.

Everyone knows that sea-water is dangerous. Consumed in large quantities it causes death by nephritis (inflammation of the kidneys). What, then, is to be done? The answer lies in a study of the composition of water. The most important constituent is sodium chloride, or common salt. I therefore made up my mind that I would consume the permissible daily intake of salt by swallowing it in sea-water. This meant that I could drink about a pint and a half of sea-water a day. The chief thing I had to worry about was its effect on the Malpighian corpuscles. These form the first filter in the kidneys and have to work hardest when there is an abnormal concentration of mineral salts. The question was how long the corpuscles could continue to work without damage. As far as I could make out, this was about five days, after which the danger of nephritis became acute.

It may be asked, what about the other chemicals in sea-water? France is famous for its mineral springs. But a quart of Salies water contains as much magnesium chloride ($MgCl_2$) as the amount of sea-water I was considering; a quart of Montmireil water holds as much magnesium sulphate ($MgSO_4$); a quart of Contrexéville water holds as much calcium sulphate ($CaSO_4$); a quart of Bourbon water holds as much potassium chloride (KCl); and lastly, a quart of Vichy *Grande Grille* water holds as much calcium carbonate ($CaCO_3$).

The water problem, therefore, seemed to be solved. The next thing to be considered in detail was the intake of food. I had to devise a diet which would provide me with the necessary number of calories, paying due attention to the three main classes of foods: proteins, fats and carbohydrates.

The table showing the chemical analysis of fish proves that as far as quantity is concerned, ample proteins are available. But the problem is complicated by the fact that the human organism makes highly selective demands and has to have a certain type of protein. One variety, called the amino-acids, is absolutely essential, and there is no substitute for it. All types of protein are to be found in fish, and the table shows the distribution in different species of the ten amino-acids which chiefly concern us here:

AMINO-ACID CONTENT OF VARIOUS FISH
Expressed in parts per ten thousand by weight

AMINO-ACID

	Arginine	Histidine	Isoleucine	Leucine	Lysine	Methionine	Phenylalanine	Threonine	Tryptophan	Valine
Mackerel	5·8	3·8	5·2	7·2	8·1	2·7	3·5	4·9	1·0	5·4
Herring	5·5	2·4	4·9	7·1	7·8	2·7	3·4	4·4	0·8	5·0
Sardine	5·1	4·7	4·6	7·2	8·4	2·8	3·7	4·3	1·0	5·2
Tunny	5·3	5·7	4·7	7·2	8·3	2·8	3·5	4·5	1·0	5·1
Shrimp	9·4	2·2	5·3	8·5	8·5	3·4	4·5	4·1	1·0	5·1

One part per ten thousand corresponds to approximately one-sixth of an ounce in a hundredweight. Thus, for example, a hundredweight of mackerel contains about one ounce of arginine.

On the other hand, there are certain types of protein of which I had to beware, particularly the ureides and purine bases. These are only present in quantity in the cartilaginous fishes, such as rays and sharks, which I would have to treat with extreme circumspection.

As far as fats were concerned, the only question was to know whether I would find phospholipids; that is to say, fats containing phosphorus, such as lecithin. (Egg-yolks are normally an important source.) Abundant fats are available in all fish.

Then came the decisive factor, that of carbohydrates and sugar. As far as the human being is concerned, these come from two sources, exogenous, that is to say consumed in food, or endogenous, manufactured by the body itself. There seemed few enough external sources of supply. Where was I to find sugar in the sea? It existed in quantity in the planktonic plants, but was it of a type which could be assimilated by the human organism?

The carbohydrates fall into three main groups:

1 The monosaccharides, which can be assimilated as they are, characterized by the fact that their molecule contains six carbon atoms (C_6). The most typical is glucose.

2 The disaccharides, with twelve atoms of carbon (C_{12}) such as saccharose, i.e. cane or beet sugar, which cannot be digested as they are but which go through a process of hydrolysis during digestion and split into two molecules of C_6 sugar.

3 The polysaccharides, carbohydrates characterized by eighteen or more carbon atoms in multiples of six in the

B

molecule. Many carbohydrates of this group, such as cellulose, cannot be absorbed by the organism and pass through it unchanged, as they cannot be hydrolysed into the assimilable C_6 components. Unfortunately these indigestible carbohydrates are the only ones to be found in plankton.

The livers of many fish generate glucose, but if I ate too much liver I risked making myself very ill through an excess of two indispensable but very dangerous substances, vitamin A and vitamin D. It therefore seemed that I was going to have to rely on my own body to manufacture the necessary carbohydrates. In normal circumstances the human organism is capable of doing this, providing it has a sufficient supply of meat, fat – and a considerable quantity of water. I was in a vicious circle and only practical experience could give the real answer. I had one encouraging example, that of the Eskimos, who for six months of the polar winter eat only meat and fat and drink melted sea-water ice, without seeming to suffer any serious consequences to their digestions.

I still needed minute quantities of certain other substances, the famous vitamins. Infinitesimal as the amounts involved are, their absence can cause serious illness – the deficiency diseases or avitaminoses. Too much of vitamins can have equally serious effects, resulting in hypervitaminoses. Four of them, vitamins A, B, C and D, are absolutely essential, and it is not possible to do without them, even for a short time. For the remainder the margin of safety is considerably wider.

Vitamin A and vitamin D, as I have noted, are extremely abundant in fish oil (I do not need to remind readers of their experiences as children with cod liver oil). Vitamins B_1 and B_2 are abundantly present in the flesh of fish in which, however, as far as I know, no one has ever detected any trace of vitamin B_{12}, the anti-pernicious anaemia factor. The margin of safety in this case is again quite wide, although the anaemic state in which I finally arrived would seem to indicate that vitamin B_{12} is only found at sea in very limited quantities.

Even with these considerations out of the way, there remained that scourge of sailors through the ages, scurvy. This is a deficiency disease due to the absence of vitamin C, present in fresh fruit, green vegetables and plant life in general. How was I to solve this problem?

My reasoning was this: animals are divided into two types, those that manufacture their own ascorbic acid (vitamin C), and those which take it in the form of food. Now the whale is one of the animals which has to find an outside source for its ascorbic acid and it feeds exclusively on plankton or on the minute crustaceans which themselves feed on plankton. It therefore seemed certain that plankton would provide my source of vitamin C, and this I verified by chemical analysis.

There seemed every possibility of making up a balanced diet. I had my vitamins A, B, C and D and, as far as their calorie content was concerned, all the proteins and fats I needed. There was only one worry, and that a vital one: would I be able to find enough water to ensure my sugar balance?

CHAPTER III

EQUIPMENT

∽ ∽ ∽ ∽ ∽ ∽ ∽ ∽ ∽ ∽ ∽

I SOON realized that it would be quite easy, statistics in hand, to convince the scientists, but that winning over the sailors would be a different matter. At any mention of my work they invariably replied: 'That's all very well in theory. It may make sense in a laboratory, but it'll be quite another thing at sea, take my word for it.'

There was still one overwhelming factor to be taken into consideration: how to defeat the greatest killer of them all, despair. It formed no part of the study of nutrition, but if drink is more important than food, instilling confidence is more important than drink. Thirst kills more quickly than hunger, but despair is a greater danger than thirst. 'What I will is fate,' as Milton wrote. I had to take into account the whole question of morale.

Who is most likely to suffer disaster at sea, the scientist or the sailor, the doctor or the fisherman? Here my doctor's training took over from my training as a physiologist, and I realized that practical evidence was necessary. If my theory was to be something more than a hypothesis, if it was to serve some real purpose, it was essential to reduce the experiment to human terms in an actual sea voyage. I had to find some way of isolating myself on the ocean for a period of between one and three months. The route I chose must have favourable winds and currents, but be unfrequented, so that we would not be tempted to board any of the ships we met.

Only by some such exploit could we fire imaginations with the proof that life can be sustained far from land.

I started to read accounts of freak voyages, particularly by those who had sailed alone. Incomparably the best work on the subject is that of my friend Jean Merrien, *Les Navigateurs Solitaires*. It needs no detailed comment here, but it makes two things clear: to attract attention it was necessary for me to cross one of the great oceans (the Atlantic seemed the most suitable); and if a voyage was to last two months without there being too much temptation to abandon it, it would be best to follow the north-east trade wind and repeat two of the journeys – the second and the fourth – made by Christopher Columbus from Spain, via the Canaries, past the Cape Verde Islands to the West Indies. This would avoid the main trade routes, which pass to the north for North America and the West Indies, and to the south for South America. It would also pass between the Sargasso Sea and the Doldrums, where we would risk certain disaster without benefiting anybody.

Life at Monaco was extremely busy. I spent whole days in the library examining the index cards file by file and extracting with the help of M. Comet, the librarian, my supply of books for the week. Almost every day I went out in one of the boats belonging to the Museum, the *Pisa* or the *Eider*, and pressed a great variety of fish in an attempt to obtain the maximum quantity of liquid, paying particular attention to the taste. I discovered that the best instrument for this purpose was a simple fruit press.

Gradually I accustomed myself to the diet I would be following and grew more confident as the results proved satisfactory. In the laboratory at least, it seemed that my theory was completely sound. By a miracle, I had managed to keep my project more or less secret, although in this I may have been helped by the polite disbelief and benevolent incredulity of those who knew about it. I was yet to learn that I was the only person who really believed in what I was doing.

Little by little, the tentative date we had fixed for our departure was postponed. At first there were to be three of us, van Hemsbergen, our sponsor and myself. Then we became five and, finally, six. At one point we had decided to use a ship's lifeboat, but later our sponsor took up a really extraordinary craft. Our experience with it did a lot towards turning me into a 'lone voyager'.

Our Dutch patron had suddenly made up his mind to employ for our experiment a sort of Polynesian cata-maran, consisting of two hulls supporting a deck – not much more than a glorified water scooter, except that it had a sail. He sent us a prototype, which had been designed – and well designed – exclusively as a seaside plaything, and suggested that we should try to get to Corsica and back in it.

Van Hemsbergen and I spent several days playing around with this ridiculous craft in the harbour, to the intense amusement of the onlookers, and then had it towed out to sea one fine morning towards the end of November. A slight breeze sprang up at about eleven o'clock and the catamaran fairly scudded over the waves. We had turned for home when one of the lee-boards broke. It should be explained that the two hulls were open so that one could sit in them; it was rather like sitting in a canoe. We had made no attempt to cover them in, even though they shipped quite a lot of water, because we wanted to test the craft's stability. As we could no longer keep head on into the sea, the inevitable soon happened, a wave broke into one of the pontoons and the whole thing turned turtle. We were well out into the bay of Monte Carlo and the wind was carrying us towards Cap Martin. We both reached the shore in the end, myself swimming and Jean towed in. The police even got mixed up in the affair, as I had scraped my thigh on the sharp rocks and they received a report that a naked, bleeding man had been seen lurking about in the woods. It was clear that I was not going to become a voluntary castaway without a few involuntary experiences first of all.

This episode should have been enough to prove to our sponsor the futility of this particular line of investigation. But, on the contrary, he drew up ambitious plans for a large catamaran nearly fifty feet long with a cabin and a galley. It was clear that we were developing different conceptions of both ends and means. Whenever I ventured a few mild suggestions and protests I was told that it was essential to give the expedition an international character, that several boats would probably take part, that there was still plenty of time and that it was even envisaged to sail round the world. The plans became increasingly visionary, until it seemed that we had completely lost sight of the basic problem of the castaway.

In my own mind I slowly built up an obstinate resolution to abide by our original plans, to work only with this object in view, and then to present my colleagues with a *fait accompli*. I was sure that once everything was ready, vacillating minds would be made up and the expedition would really revert to its original purpose. I was told that everything would be ready for about May or June and I decided to make my plans accordingly. Then we would start, with the blessing, I felt sure, of our patron.

By the end of March, my laboratory studies were to all

intents and purposes finished. My next door neighbour in the laboratory was Dr S. K. Kon, of Reading University, who had come to Monaco to study the family of minute planktonic crustaceans that form the principal food of whales, and which are to be found on the surface of the sea between Mentone and Cap Martin. Dr Kon suggested that he should introduce me to one or two experts who would be able to complete my information. I therefore paid a quick visit to England, where, thanks to him and to Dr Magee, of the Ministry of Health, I was put in touch with representatives of the Navy and Air Force, of whom one, Dr Whittingham, became my good friend. They all made both their interest and (when they had any) their doubts very clear. Dr Whittingham also met our patron and paid us a short visit in Monaco. My only regret was that on two occasions I missed meeting Professor MacCance, the Cambridge plankton specialist.

My journey was not without some curious repercussions. When I was passing through the Customs at Calais, one of the inspectors said to me:

'Another channel crossing, eh?'

I smiled: 'Oh! no, this time it's the Atlantic.'

He gave a short, incredulous laugh, but on reflection must have said to himself: 'After all why not? . . .' and passed on the tip to a British newspaper.

Thus it was that the press started to take an interest in us. One day a journalist came to interview me at the laboratory in Monaco and a whole sequence of reports began to appear, many of them grossly distorting the facts. Without realizing it, I had touched off 'publicity', and the reports became increasingly grotesque. I was referred to as 'Professor' Bombard with all sorts of learned titles. . . . It all acquired the tone of the worst form of publicity campaign and seriously interfered with my work. The only good result was the stream of volunteers who offered their services, making it clear that there was no danger of my lacking company. Still counting on van Hemsbergen, I only needed one more member to complete the crew. One day a tall Englishman, red-haired, and of the true phlegmatic type, came to place himself, his sextant and his boat at my disposal. His name was Herbert Muir-Palmer, a naturalized citizen of Panama, and better known as Jack Palmer. A first-class seaman and navigator, he had sailed from Panama across the Atlantic, through the Mediterranean to Cairo and then, in company with his wife, from Cairo to Monaco, in a little ten-metre yacht, the *Hermione*, touching at Cyprus and Tobruk and passing through the Straits of Messina. He had been at Monaco for a year or so, and was short of money, like so many of these lone sailors. I told him all about our plans: how two or three of us wanted to place ourselves in the situation of shipwrecked survivors in a lifeboat or life-raft, without food or water, in order to prove to the world that survival was possible in such conditions. He asked me to give him a few hours to think it over, not wanting to commit himself lightly, and then came back and said:

'Dr Bombard, I am your man.'

I liked him better every day and was overjoyed with my 'find'. But we were still safely on land. In spite of myself I could not help thinking: 'What will he be like when we get really hungry? What happens if we fall out between ourselves? I know Hemsbergen's reactions, but what about Palmer?'

It was because of this that we finally decided to make a trial run in the Mediterranean instead of setting off straight away from Tangier or Casablanca. This almost land-locked sea, so deceptively like a lake, would test both men and equipment. The worse it behaved the greater service it would render. We would know all the

*B

difficulties confronting us and would then be able to
challenge the Atlantic.

I was negotiating with the people who had made the
Hitch Hiker for a similar craft, somewhat larger, and the
discussions went slowly. In the meantime I continued to
receive countless offers from volunteers and had to put
up with a cloud of newspapermen. Some of the letters I
received unfolded the most delightful and bizarre ideas.
One prospective crew-member tried to strengthen his
case by offering to allow himself to be eaten if the experiment failed. Another wrote to say that he had already
tried to commit suicide three times; he asked if he might
come with us because he thought I had hit on a workable
method of achieving his aim. Yet a third proposed that I
should take his mother-in-law as a passenger, suggesting
that my efforts at life-saving could well start by rescuing
a marriage which was being wrecked by the person in
question. Another correspondent asked how he could
irrigate his garden with sea-water, since I claimed it had
no deleterious effects. Of course, there were other
suggestions of a more reasonable kind, such as offers of
experimental equipment, which it was suggested I should
test.

On 15th May, a Thursday, I received a telephone call
from Jean-Luc de Carbuccia, who has become my close
friend, offering to publish the book I was to write about
my experiences and proposing a contract which made the
expedition more or less self-sufficient and would leave
my wife without material worries. Two days later I went
to Paris and, after a last heated argument with the maker,
took over the craft which was to become L'Hérétique.
Triumphant, I returned to Monaco with my personal
transatlantic liner. At long last the expedition was about
to start, just when everyone seemed to have ceased
believing in it. I sent telegrams to van Hemsbergen and

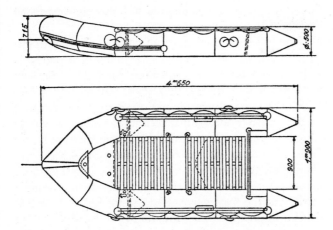

our patron. The latter arrived the evening before we were due to set off, saying: 'This is the best day of my life, not only my birthday, but the start of the adventure. Van Hemsbergen has been detained, but I have come to take his place.'

I then had to convince him that his twenty-five stone could not possibly be accommodated in such a frail vessel and that it would be a much greater service to the expedition if he would stay behind and organize the next stage. Palmer and I were ready to leave the following day, the 24th, and the designer of our boat, the well-known airman, Debroutelle, was attending to the last details of our inflatable dinghy in the harbour of Monaco.

It was a sort of horseshoe-shaped inflatable rubber sausage, some fifteen feet long and six feet wide and seemed the perfect piece of equipment for such an expedition as ours. The open end was closed by a wooden stern-board, over which we could trail our fishing nets and lines without causing damage by friction to the fragile rubber floats. The bottom of the boat was about three feet wide and supported a lightweight wooden deck-board.

There was not a single piece of metal in the whole construction. The floats were divided into five compartments – the curved bow, and two along each side – by hermetically sealed rubber bulkheads. An outside valve, which could be turned on and off as required, allowed air to pass from one compartment to the other. It will be seen in due course how useful this arrangement was. The deck, or bottom – it was one and the same – was practically flat, and there was a rigid keel running the length of the boat. It had a dinghy sail of about three square yards, but the mast was placed too far forward, which made it impossible to sail into the wind. However, there were two lee-boards fixed about a third of the way down the sides and these gave the craft a certain degree of manœuvrability, although in practice I used them little except when approaching land.

All I needed now was a sailing permit. One would have thought it a simple enough formality, but in this case it turned out to be extremely difficult, and at one moment it looked as if the whole project would collapse through the lack of this one piece of paper. A few days earlier I had been given an unpleasant surprise; the local court in the north of France had ruled, in my absence, that I should pay a suspended fine of two thousand francs for breaking the regulations concerning navigation on the high seas. Wishing to defend myself, I jumped into a train to go and oppose the finding.

◦   ◦   ◦   ◦   ◦   ◦   ◦   ◦   ◦

The second act of what I have called the Comic Interlude took place in the imposing surroundings of a court of petty sessions. I was charged with having used on the high seas, without a navigation permit, a craft designed only for use off the beach.

My turn came to speak:

'Your Honour, I must say I find it curious to be alone here on this charge as I was only a passenger in a boat, whose owner was on board. I should also like to ask whether I would have been granted a navigation permit if I had asked for it?'

'It would neither have been refused nor granted, and is not necessary in this case.'

At this point the prosecutor jumped up like a jack-in-the-box and launched into a violent diatribe, although he had not said a word up till then.

'Your Honour,' he said, 'the Court should know that the accused is a public danger, whose bad example might well cause loss of life amongst the young people in these parts. He has already been fined two thousand francs in default. As he has committed two offences, there should be a double fine.'

'Sir, I am in the process of conducting an experiment which may be of world-wide importance,' I tried to explain. 'In the interests of all concerned I hope you will not find it necessary to fine me.'

The prosecutor broke in again. 'It is quite clear that the accused is an irresponsible hoaxer,' he said. 'This experiment only exists in his own imagination.'

After due deliberation, the Court imposed two suspended fines of a thousand francs, one on each charge. There was no time in which to enter an appeal, so I returned to Monaco.

◌   ◌   ◌   ◌   ◌   ◌   ◌   ◌   ◌

When I got back from this hearing I received another visitor, whose ideas were in due course to imperil the whole expedition. He was a good-looking fellow in his early thirties, typical of a certain type of journalist, full of energy and vulgarity. He started the interview by asking:

'Do you have a radio transmitter?'

'No.'

'Well count yourself lucky, because I am going to see that you get one.'

I looked at my benefactor open-mouthed, hardly able to believe in this unexpected offer. Then he went on:

'We are very much interested in your experiment. However, you must realize that putting a radio transmitter-receiver in a craft such as yours presents a number of technical problems. We would like to go into them with you; will you agree?'

I shook hands with him effusively.

'It may not be easy to get a broadcasting licence from the Principality, but try and give us all the notice you can and we will bring the equipment immediately.'

'You do realize', I said, 'that I would then need the set as quickly as possible – it is going to take a little while to install it.'

'Leave it to us,' he answered, and off he went.

Delighted with this new development, I put in the necessary application to the Monaco administration, with a request that it should be given priority. I received the licence on 23rd May, but I had been given advance notice and was able to pass the word to the reporter on 20th May.

While in Paris on 16th May I had told Jean-Luc all about this offer, but instead of becoming as excited as I was, he was slightly discouraging.

'Have you any idea of the complications involved?' he said. 'It would need a professional expert, or at least a

highly gifted amateur, to maintain contact across two
thousand miles of ocean with such a tiny set.'

This had, in fact, occurred to me and I had already
tried to impress on my reporter friend that I was totally
ignorant of anything to do with radio.

'All the more reason for your having one,' he had said.

Jean-Luc, not sharing my confidence, thought over the
problem, and after I had left Paris he got in touch with a
friend of his, named Jean Ferré, who was connected with
the French Transmitting Network. I was not worrying. I
had yet to learn that I was going to get no radio – but
that by way of compensation I should win two good
friends.

On 22nd May Jean Ferré telephoned me from Paris.
His curiosity was only equalled by his indignation.
'What sort of valves do you have?' he asked me. 'What
type of aerial? What is your source of power? What wave-
lengths will you work on? What is the make of the
receiver?'

It was all Greek to me and I could only stammer in
reply that I had complete confidence in the people who
were giving me the equipment.

'But experts would expect to give months of study to
this problem,' he went on. 'Radio amateurs like me, with
modest equipment and not operating under the best of
conditions, need at least a fortnight, even when the sets
are installed, to put them in full working order. Today
is the 22nd and you want to leave on the 24th without
as much as having seen your equipment yet. You must
be crazy . . .' and he hung up.

Thoroughly shaken, I rang up my journalist friend.
'Please hurry up, I am leaving on the 24th,' I said. 'We
know that perfectly well, dear Dr Bombard, just have
confidence in us,' he replied.

On the morning of the 23rd I went to meet Carbuccia

and Ferré at the station. As a form of introduction, the latter was brandishing a typed document:

> The President of the French Transmitting Network has the honour to present to Doctor Bombard Monsieur Jean Ferré F9OV, with a view to studying the technical problems involved in maintaining a radio link during his voyage. M. Ferré will inform Doctor Bombard of the steps that have been taken to co-operate with this sporting and scientific experiment of such interest to radio amateurs.
>
> Signed: Marcheville F8NH.

(Perhaps it should be pointed out that every amateur transmitter is allotted a call sign by the French postal administration. In France these signs begin with an F, while those of Monaco begin with 3A9.)

I was astonished at the official turn things had taken. It was then explained to me that I had become a special case, that what I was going to do had never been attempted before and that very special conditions were attached to the equipment I needed. First of all, it would need a hermetically sealed container to protect it against sea-water and condensation, and this container must not be too heavy for the boat. It would need an absolutely foolproof source of power and must be capable of working with any type of aerial and on a variety of wave-lengths. It would need either a very experienced operator or a highly complicated set of controls.

Jean Ferré spared me no details: 'Working on short waves is a tricky business. You might need to work between ten and forty metres to ensure contact. In certain conditions even a hundred-kilowatt transmitter cannot be heard, and yours will only have the power of ten watts.'

There was only one solution, he told me, and that was

to enlist the help of the radio 'hams'. There are more than two hundred thousand of them scattered round the globe, with long experience of picking up feeble signals. The French Transmitting Network would send them a notice about me and there would always be someone on watch day and night. I could only stutter my thanks at the thought of this immense host of well-wishers who would be on the look-out for me.

'I must have a good look at your equipment', said Jean Ferré, 'before I can tell whether they'll be able to pick you up at all.' There was still no sign of it or its donors. Jean Ferré rang them up himself. 'Do not worry, the stuff is on its way,' he was told.

'Have you any idea of the problems facing you?'

'Yes, of course.'

'What sort of aerial have you in mind?'

'We are going to fix it on the mast.'

'The mast of L'Hérétique is not more than six feet high. An aerial there would have no range at all.'

There was silence from the other end.

'Why don't you use a balloon or a kite?' Jean Ferré suggested.

'Good idea.'

'What is the make of receiver?'

'Everything is in hand.'

'What frequency are you using?'

'Thirty megacycles.'

We sent off this information by telegram to M. de Marcheville. His reply came back immediately: 'Thirty Mc/s frequency of WWV. Do not understand.'

We did not understand either. WWV is the station of the National Bureau of Standards in Washington, which floods the ether with its hundred-kilowatt transmitter. Quite clearly, my own little set was not going to be able to compete with it on the same wave-length.

We telephoned my benefactors again.

'Don't worry, everything will be all right,' they insisted.

That evening, Friday the 23rd, one of their representatives arrived in Monaco. 'I have come to prepare the ground,' he said. 'The equipment will arrive tomorrow.'

We told him all about the problems involved and they staggered him.

'Nonsense, it's inconceivable,' he said, but not one of us could raise a smile.

I had now become convinced that the radio idea was hopeless. I thought of ringing up to say that I would leave without it and that they should call the whole thing off. But even then I hesitated. Perhaps after all they had thought out all the problems, and why should I nullify their efforts?

My wife was getting anxious too. 'Do you think we are going to be able to keep in touch with Alain?' she asked Jean Ferré. He did not answer. He was pacing up and down like a lion in a cage, thinking of the hundreds of hours needed to adjust an amateur's transmitter, and of all the experts a commercial undertaking would employ for the purpose. And here were we without as much as having seen a piece of wire.

We had decided to sail on the 24th at three o'clock in the afternoon. At eleven o'clock in the morning a group of people arrived with the equipment, my reporter friend among them. He buttonholed Jean Ferré. 'Who do I negotiate the exclusive rights with?' he asked. Jean looked at him with blank incomprehension. 'Exclusive rights? What exclusive rights? Wasn't the idea to help two people who are risking their lives on behalf of shipwrecked sailors?'

'The exclusive broadcasting rights. You understand of

course. I can sell them to the BBC – perhaps even to the Americans, if I have the rights.'

While this was going on I was looking at the set. The transmitter was a simple chassis without any protective covering, such as one might install with infinite precautions on a laboratory table. The receiver was a simple commercial battery model. Only the generator was a piece of high quality equipment.

'What about the aerial?' I asked.

'The best we have been able to manage in the time is a kite,' I was told.

At midday Jean called a meeting at my room in the hotel. 'On behalf of the French Transmitting Network, which has asked me to give my opinion in this matter, I must state without equivocation that there is no possibility of maintaining contact between the dinghy and land with this equipment,' he said. 'First of all, the sets are not protected against sea-water; then it would take an expert to use them. The first shock or the loss of the aerial would mean complete breakdown. Everyone would think the expedition had been lost at sea, and that would only cause unnecessary anxiety. Neither Bombard nor Palmer has any knowledge of morse and there is no means of voice transmission.'

'Dr Bombard,' the others replied, 'you have nothing to worry about. This gentleman here is doubtless full of good intentions but lacks experience. Have confidence in us, we will keep watch for your messages.'

My friends were appalled and my wife consumed with worry. I held a council of war with Palmer. I knew the radio would never work, but after all what did it matter? A month earlier I had not dreamed of having one, and in any case, a castaway would be unlikely to be equipped with a radio transmitter. There was nothing to worry about. As the wind was in the wrong quarter, however, we put off our departure for twenty-four hours, so that they did at least have a day in which to instal the set.

I shall never forget the last sentence of the radio commentator describing the scene from the launch which towed us out to sea on Sunday the 25th. 'We will ask your news in the form of questions. Please signal a dot for yes and a dash for no. Goodbye, Doctor. Remember dot yes, dash no, dot yes, dash no . . .'

I would like to put on record the events of the day that preceded our departure. Once the press had started to interest itself in our expedition, we had been increasingly assailed by journalists and the curious. I now have nothing to learn about the art of the news photographer trying to find the best angle for his shot. My work had been hampered for weeks and I always seemed to have a newspaperman at my elbow. The twenty-four hours before our departure became a circus. I could not even walk along the street with my wife without being tapped on the shoulder by some complete stranger who asked me to stand there and kiss her so that he could get a good photograph.

This wave of publicity was unfortunate as far as our departure was concerned. Certainly the press has a right to keep the public informed, and quite often it is not so much a sober account of the facts as the human anecdote which interests the great mass of readers. But the whole spirit of the expedition was falsified in the eyes of a number of people and discredited in the minds of others. The departure had to be made 'sensational', so everyone lost sight of the reasons for our preliminary canter in the Mediterranean: the testing of equipment and crew. Our 'dress rehearsal' was in danger of being judged as a first night; the least failure in doing what we had said we were going to do (or – worse – had been reported as saying we were going to do) might discredit the whole expedition. No attempt was made to understand that we had everything to learn and that we still had to work out the minute day-to-day routine on board. We were presented as the stars of a dramatic situation. This false picture given by the press was particularly dangerous in view of the fact that we were setting out to challenge generally accepted principles and the dictates of common sense.

I was a heretic on several counts. We were going to try and reach, in a craft not considered capable of navigation, a destination determined in advance. This first heresy particularly affected the professional seamen and navigators who assured us that we would never get further than the Îles d'Hyères. More particularly, I was attacking the general belief that it was impossible to live on the resources of the sea alone and that sea-water was undrinkable. Moreover (to repeat the comments made in one of the more reputable publications), when even experienced seamen never felt absolutely confident of their ability to combat the dangers of sea, winds and currents, a rank amateur was not hesitating to trust his companion's life and his own to a ridiculous cockleshell whose design had not even been approved by a qualified marine surveyor.

For these reasons, and many others, I named our ship L'Hérétique.

Fortunately we still enjoyed the support of many persons in authority. Due to the personal intervention of the Under-Secretary of State at the Ministry of Naval Affairs, M. Jacques Gavini, I was granted my navigation permit. Thus it was that L'Hérétique was able to wear the French flag all the way across the Atlantic.

PART TWO

MEDITERRANEAN

5°W   0°

F R

SPAIN

• Madrid

40°N

Scale of Geographical miles
50   100   150   200   250

Estimated position 1st Ju

COLUMBRETE

Valencia

8th Ju

Ibiza

13th July

Alicante

MEDITER

Gibraltar
Ceuta
Tangier

5°W   0°

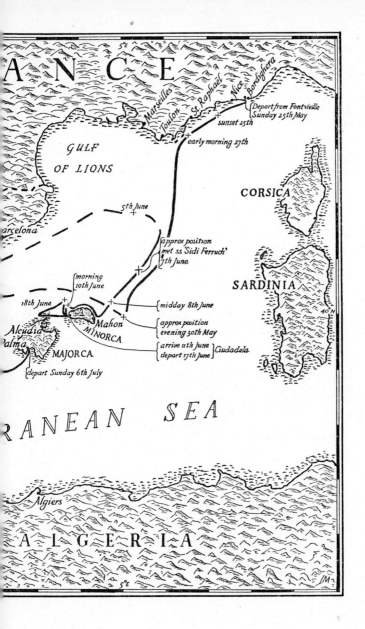

FRANCE

GULF OF LIONS

Marseilles

Toulon

St. Raphaël

Nice

Bordighera

Depart from Fontvieille
Sunday 25th May

sunset 25th

early morning 27th

CORSICA

5th June

Barcelona

approx position
met s.s. 'Sidi Ferruch'
7th June

SARDINIA

40°N

morning
10th June

18th June

midday 8th June

Alcudia
Palma

Mahon
MINORCA

approx position
evening 30th May

MAJORCA

arrive 11th June
depart 17th June } Ciudadela

depart Sunday 6th July

MEDITERRANEAN SEA

Algiers

ALGERIA

5°E

CHAPTER IV

DEPARTURE

∽ ∽ ∽ ∽ ∽ ∽ ∽ ∽ ∽ ∽ ∽

WE ALL met at dawn in the little harbour of Fontvieille. Harassed by importunate newspapermen, to whose questions I replied to the best of my ability, I supervised the loading of equipment into the dinghy. A large crowd had started to gather, but we had no intention of setting off until about three o'clock in the afternoon, when the wind conditions were normally at their best. The group of electricians worked feverishly to put the wireless transmitter in order, encouraged by a chorus of advice from the local amateurs of Monte Carlo and Nice. At about two o'clock an official arrived to seal the jerry-cans of emergency water which we were carrying in case the experiment ended in disaster. While we were being pestered by photographers, a messenger from the Museum of Oceanography came to tell me that the Museum's boat was not available to tow us out to sea on a Saturday or Sunday.

This point should be explained. The dinghy was incapable of sailing into the wind. In order to become castaways, we had to start as far away from the coast as possible, as otherwise an unfavourable wind would have driven us straight back again. It was therefore necessary, as with the Kon-Tiki, for us to be towed out about a dozen miles off the coast. Fortunately there was an American cruiser anchored in the bay, and its captain agreed to lend us one of his launches for the purpose.

By this time the crowd had become immense. The wind had veered to the south-west and was almost certain to drive us ashore again if we set off. The spectators were clearly tired of waiting and were impatient to see us leave. The captain of the American cruiser agreed to lend us the launch again the next morning and we decided to put off our departure till then. Jack seemed to think that the wind would veer in our favour, a prognostication confirmed by the local meteorological station, which, for once, got its forecast right. As soon as the crowd learnt of our decision there were loud cries of complaint; even some of the journalists started to grumble, furious at having wasted their day for nothing. Then a big fellow, dressed in sort of cowboy style, with a wide-brimmed hat, came up to me out of the crowd, and gave me this piece of advice:

'Young man, I know something about this business, I have just got back from South America. There is no point in being squeamish. If your companion dies on the way, don't throw him overboard. Eat him. Anything serves as food; I have even eaten shark.'

'Thank you,' I replied politely, 'I will follow your advice.'

Then I went back to the hotel to get some rest.

We were back again in the harbour at about half past four in the morning. The crowd had reduced itself to our own friends. The atmosphere was completely different, everything had suddenly become real. We were no longer a circus act, but two people leaving on a long and arduous voyage. I suddenly felt buoyed up; we were really off. Ginette was there, Jean, Jean-Luc, a few reporters, together with the technicians. Jack and I ordered a last cup of white coffee and a ham roll. When these were brought, our mood had changed and we refused to eat them. After all, whether we stopped eating then or a few

hours later was immaterial. We had no idea how much
we were to regret our quixotic gesture during the long
days of fast that we were to endure.

Five o'clock. With true naval punctuality, the American
cruiser's launch swept into the little harbour. In spite of
the early hour, the captain himself had come along to
direct operations. Everything was ready. Jack and I
climbed silently into L'Hérétique. We had barely exchanged
a couple of words the whole morning.

'Ready?' shouted the captain.

'Yes.'

'Let's go.'

Slowly the launch took up the tow and made for the
open sea. We sat opposite each other on the inflated
floats, our legs dangling inboard. The sea was quite
choppy, giving us a foretaste of what bad weather was
going to be like. The waves seemed short and unpredictable, running irregularly and breaking continuously.
The launch rolled and pitched, but the dinghy, in spite
of the sea, remained remarkably steady, which seemed a
good omen. She rode the waves well, with very little
motion and made light weather of it. Everyone in the
launch was hunched over and hanging on to something
to keep on their feet; every now and again the clapper of
the launch's bell swung with the swell and sent out a
sharp peal. With our hands completely free, Jack and I
waved goodbye to those we left on shore. Right from
the start, we felt, L'Hérétique was proving superior to the
orthodox.

Ginette was in the launch, making brave efforts to
smile, but her dark sun-glasses hid the tears I knew were
in her eyes. A few hundred yards out we were joined by
two or three other craft and our departure took on the
aspect of a regatta. It was certainly modest enough, but
later, at the start of each new lap of our journey, the

partisans of heresy were to become more numerous. At this stage our true purpose was barely understood.

Although we waved and smiled, Jack and I already had the sensation that we were well on our way and no longer belonged to the world we had just left. We were already becoming part of our frail craft, the only home we were to know for many a long day and the centre of our universe. The sea round us was covered with white horses, soon to become familiar companions, and as their spray started to soak us, the launch sounded its bell. At a sign from Jack the tow was dropped.

We waved and shouted our goodbyes. The accompanying craft circled round us a couple of times and we responded mechanically to their parting gestures. Although they did not realize it, our fellow human beings had become strangers. The sense of adventure separated them from us more surely than any wall. We had a sudden feeling that we had parted company with mankind. Our new life at sea had become more real and tangible than our relationships with those still so close. 'Oh, do go away!' would have been the only words with meaning that we could have shouted, but although we may have thought them, we did not even whisper.

Slowly the other boats disappeared from view. Soon we were completely alone, isolated in a strange new element in the cockleshell which was our only support. Fear, the enemy which was to attack me so often during the coming seven months, laid its clammy hand on me for the first time, as if the last boat to disappear from sight had made way for it. The sensation only lasted a moment, a surface scratch compared with the deep wounds it had yet to cause me. We were to know the feeling well, not this light touch of fear at the moment of departure, but the panic revolt of body and soul terrified

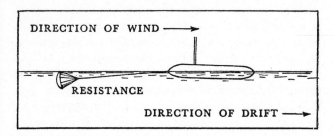

by the elements, as if the whole universe had combined in one dreadful menace.

The wind started to blow in strong gusts and spray hid the still sleeping land. We could just see the top of the 'Tête de Chien' and the Italian cliffs by Bordighera. All that remained of the boats which had brought us out were their white wakes on the horizon. We were face to face with the unknown. We had conjured up visions of this solitude for so long that it seemed like some strange gift one had dreamed about for years and that was suddenly being presented in tangible form. The sea and the wind we knew, and the sound of the waves, but this was our first true rendezvous with them. Now that we were here, everything seemed to fall into place and all was well.

Jack and I sat in an oppressive silence. It seemed as if the whole future was weighing down on our thoughts. We did not hoist the sail immediately as Jack was afraid it might part in the strong wind and he wanted to test its strength and that of the mast by degrees. In order not to be driven back to Nice we used, for the first time, our floating sea anchor. This was a device much in favour in the days of sail, and resuscitated for modern use by the famous Captain Voss. It can consist of any half-submerged object streamed from the bow on a length of rope. Its purpose is to keep the head of a ship into the wind in order to meet the waves in the most favourable position. In a storm all the sails are taken in and the ship drifts before the wind, with the sea anchor acting as a brake. This prevents the boat turning beam on to the wind and risking a capsize. Our sea anchor consisted of a little parachute which filled under the pressure of water, thus slowing down our progress exactly as an air parachute slows an airman descending from the skies. In due course, in order to support my theories, which demanded the minimum amount of equipment on board, I used my sea anchor for other purposes as well, such as catching plankton.

With the anchor out, L'Hérétique turned obediently to face the Italian coast. The sun rose slowly, dissipating the mist and showing the dangerous coast looming near. We had to get as much sea room as possible in order to pass the various points and promontories which stuck out like traps along our route. The most important of these were Cap Ferrat, Cap d'Antibes and the Lérins Islands, followed by Cap Camarat and the island of Levant, which even our least pessimistic friends had told us we would never succeed in passing. After that the coast turned north and west and we had open sea in front of us.

The wind became lighter and we hoisted our sail. This was a complicated operation as the mast was in the fore part of the boat. We had covered in the forward part of the bath-tub shaped dinghy with a tent, leaving the after part as an open deck about six feet six inches long and three feet six inches wide. We could not step on the tent to reach the bow as we would have gone right through the thin fabric, and we had to perform a tight-rope act along the floats. The return journey was even more acrobatic as there was not the mast to make for. I usually laid out flat, pulling myself along by my arms.

L'Hérétique started to move. I must say she made a splendid sight, sailing large with the main sheet paid right out, leaving a broad wake which, though it bore no relation to her speed, gave a fine sensation of motion. We set up a considerable backwash, the height of which we hoped would give us some indication of our speed. Later I was to judge this more nicely by the pull of the sail on the main sheet. For the time being we were probably not making more than a knot and a half, but that was better than nothing.

At about eleven o'clock, just as we were rounding Cap Ferrat, the wind died right down. It seemed it was quite a problem to cast oneself adrift. We had still hardly spoken a word and it required an effort to break the silence. Each of us was thinking of what we had left behind. It had not taken us long to begin reacting normally to events and all our memories and regrets as landsmen had soon reasserted themselves. The loved ones we had abandoned now reoccupied their accustomed place in our minds. The mood of feeling like legendary heroes had passed and we had become our normal selves again.

To pull ourselves together, we held our first council of war, each making an effort to appear calm and ordinary in the eyes of the other. The most difficult thing was to talk in a normal tone of voice, as we both had a tendency to speak very softly. It was something we had to correct because we realized that if we continued to murmur like this, the spectre of fear would take it as an invitation to assert itself.

Taking advantage of this uneventful interval, we started to work out the details of our life on board. We put out a couple of fishing lines as a step towards the next meal and then set about allotting every minute of the day in much more detail than during the long period of

c

preparation on land. The first problem was to organize the watches. Each of us was to take the tiller in turn during the day, while the other rested, as I was certain that the abnormal life we were about to lead would demand the maximum amount of sleep. The night watches were even more important. In a sea as frequented as the Mediterranean, it was essential for one of us to be on watch, so we decided that one of us would take over from eight in the evening until one in the morning, and the other from then until eight in the morning.

Everything on board was stowed where we could find it immediately, even in pitch darkness. In the bow, under the tent, protected from sea and damp in water-tight containers, we put the cameras, films, navigation books, the sextant, first-aid box, the stock of flares for use in an emergency, the sealed boxes of food and the repair kit. The compass was in its binnacle, just in front of the steersman, so that he could keep his eye on it at all times.

No fish had nibbled at the hooks by lunch time, but during the morning we had replaced the sea anchor by the plankton net, which not only performed the same function, but collected a supply of food, adequate in composition if not in quantity. In about an hour the net caught two full tablespoons of a sort of pap, by no means unpleasant to the taste and quite filling, if not particularly appetizing to look at. For the greater part it consisted of animal plankton, almost exclusively copepods, with a taste like crab or lobster purée, really quite a feast. Jack watched me eat my share with a somewhat doubtful look, but he did not wish to appear timid and finally took a taste, rather like a lost explorer being given a meal of slug jam. To his surprise he found the dish by no means unpleasant and I discreetly enjoyed my first victory.

We had both become much calmer and as this superb late spring day progressed, our presence in this heretical craft suddenly appeared quite normal. All our anxieties disappeared. This gradual normalization, the calm after anxiety, the quick forgetting of the wrench of separation, was to become the regular pattern in the Atlantic, to a point where there seemed nothing out of the ordinary in the strange life I was leading. My theories were already finding their justification. It was just a question of the first few hours of adaptation.

It has been maintained that sea-water is laxative. It may be that the sulphates of calcium and magnesium it contains have this effect on land, when other factors are normal, but after my experiences, I assert emphatically that this is not the case at sea, a fact which certain German experiments have confirmed. Jack was much more hesitant than I was to give sea-water a trial, and preferred to await a catch of fish or a rain storm before slaking his thirst. In spite of my advice and arguments, he refused to take a drop. It was a striking example of the danger caused by habits of thought too deeply rooted, but he was not to be moved even when he saw me drinking it. While still on land he had agreed completely with my theory and fully intended to make the experiment, but once he was faced by reality, the taboo placed for so many generations on sea-water conquered his previous intentions. So there we were, literally in the same boat, one of us conforming to the inhibitions of the classic castaway and the other with his heretical ideas.

Suddenly Jack's voice broke into my thoughts:

'Alain, it is three o'clock and they will be expecting our first radio message. We might as well take advantage of the calm.'

I agreed, though we had few illusions about the result, most of them having been destroyed by Jean Ferré before our departure. We knew that our jerry-rigged set was a laboratory instrument liable to damage at the least shock, its wiring and circuits entirely at the mercy of damp. We were convinced that the thing was not going to work, but there, it was three o'clock . . . For several minutes now all round the Mediterranean, radio amateurs would have been searching the ether, ignorant of the ludicrous nature of our equipment.

'It's three o'clock,' Jack repeated.

I thought of my wife, alone in Monaco, of Radio Geneva, and of the jerry-can of water we had had to leave behind to compensate for the weight of the set. I thought of all the telephone calls my wife would be receiving about four o'clock to say, 'We have been listening for them for over an hour.' Perhaps, after all, Jean Ferré was wrong. Perhaps it was true that the set had been constructed especially for our purposes. Perhaps we were going to be able to maintain contact with land. My hopes rose. Perhaps this combination of wires and valves served some purpose after all. Surely no one would deliberately take advantage of two men engaged in such an adventure as ours.

'Jack, let's get the aerial up,' I said.

The aerial. Have you ever tried to launch a kite without moving from your chair? The experts had either overlooked this problem or had assumed that we could do it. I hope that some day I can persuade one of them to try and launch a kite with its precious aerial, as we had to, from a platform six feet long. We must both have cut ridiculous figures, lurching and stumbling with each wave. And then the kite plunged into the sea, soaked and useless. We were overcome by a sense of horror. Supposing our friends on land were still waiting after all.

'Put up the emergency aerial,' I cried. This was a steel fishing rod on a halyard. When hoisted up the mast it was about fifteen feet high, appearing not much higher than the waves, and the wire which led down from it was attached to the transmitter. I tried the pilot light, tapped the ammeter and said to Jack: 'Turn the thing.'

The generator between his knees started to make a grinding noise and a mysterious current seemed to run through everything. The valves lit up. Rather like firing my last shot, I started tapping the morse key. . . . I must have repeated the message a hundred times. I turned all the knobs, tested all the wires, put my fingers on the contacts to see if there was any sign of the expected two hundred and fifty volts. A single drop of water or some slight shock to the quartz crystal had been enough. . . .

Without saying a word, Jack had stopped turning the generator; his gaze met mine. 'It's no good,' I said, 'now we are completely alone.'

Night fell in a multi-coloured sky and the first light-house appeared on our right; it was Cap d'Antibes, which we recognized from the description in our Pilot Book. This is a volume published by the naval authorities, which gives the characteristics, by areas, of every light-house in existence. Each is different, according to the duration and frequency of the flash, its colour and grouping, and each is perfectly easy to identify.

Then the night breeze sprang up from the land and carried us out to sea. It was a factor we had counted on. Those who were convinced that a dozen hours would find us thrown back on some beach again had been proved mistaken. We had scored a decisive point which, by its very nature, gave us encouragement from the first day. Perhaps, after all, we should have been grateful to the doubters, for the triumph would otherwise have seemed less sweet.

The first night was upon us. I had drawn the first watch, until one in the morning, and we were to reverse the order the next day. This arrangement soon proved indispensable, as the first watch from eight o'clock until one proved much more tiring than the second, in spite of its being shorter.

During the day we had taken up various positions, not all of them particularly safe, but we settled down for the night with the steersman sitting next to the rudder oar, with his back resting on a Mae West, and the compass between his legs, a deliberately uncomfortable position to prevent the risk of his dropping off to sleep. His feet touched the end of the tent, which protected the sleeping partner. To make enough room for the man off watch to stretch out, we had ranged all the equipment along the left-hand side of our 'bath-tub', leaving a free space about two feet wide and nearly six feet long. The tent served as a blanket and the bags as a pillow.

Jack dropped off to sleep, but I was not the only one left awake. At nightfall the sea became a hive of activity. All its inhabitants apparently came to take a look at us and the snorts of porpoises and splashes of leaping fish round the boat peopled the night with strange phantoms, redoubtable at first, but soon familiar. The slap of the waves resolved itself into a regular murmur punctuated by occasional noises, like the voice of a soloist against a muted orchestra. '*La mer, la mer toujours recommencée, s'exprimant dans un tumulte au silence pareil.*'[1] That expresses it perfectly. The regular movement of the sea ends by seeming as silent as the summit of a high mountain. Silence and noise are always relative, and silence can be as expressive as any sound. Does not Bach, that master of orchestration, make superb use of an interval of silence in his D Minor Toccata? An organ point floating on silence.

ᴄ   ᴄ   ᴄ   ᴄ   ᴄ   ᴄ   ᴄ   ᴄ   ᴄ

[1]P. Valéry: *Cimetière Marin*.

The land breeze lasted the whole of the night and the dinghy slid slowly along. Before getting into the region of regular winds, we were relying largely on the alternation of sea and land breezes to make progress. The breeze blowing inland from the sea during the morning is followed, after a pause, by the breeze off the land in the evening, as if a fresh supply of air were being inhaled by the sea for the night. The ocean seemed to heave a great sigh every day, carrying our frail craft along on the torrent of its breath.

The phenomenon has, of course, a perfectly rational and familiar explanation: during the morning the land warms up more quickly than the sea, and the air above it rises. The colder sea air moves in to take its place, thereby forming a circuit of movement. But if the sea warms more slowly, it retains its heat longer, and during the night the air movement is reversed. What we had to do was to take advantage of the night wind and lie up during the day.

The first night showed how essential it was to keep watch. We met at least ten ships. Low in the water, our riding light was practically invisible, and certainly insufficient to ensure our safety. To meet this danger with the means on board we had the idea, whenever a ship appeared likely to pass perilously close, of shining our electric torch on the sail, thus illuminating a larger area, which must have been visible from quite a distance. I could not help feeling what a curious effect this disembodied light must cause, apparently floating between crest and trough, and I wondered if we did not revive for those who saw it some legend of the sea. We must have looked like a ghost ship. On the other hand, I may be exaggerating and it may well be that we were not noticed at all.

Finally my watch ended and I handed over to Jack,

then slept myself like an innocent until he woke me up on the morning of 26th May. At first I could not imagine where I was. It was a feeling I had not had since my childhood, the complete bewilderment of waking up in some strange hotel room. Nor was I to have it again for many months, until the morning after my arrival in the West Indies.

As we expected, the wind had veered and was edging us towards the coast. For the first time we let down our lee-boards in an attempt to hold our course with the wind on the beam. This was the most the dinghy could manage, as it was incapable of sailing into the wind. The lee-boards proved very effective, and although they reduced our speed to about one knot, we managed to keep a safe distance from the coast on a parallel course.

We started to feel very hungry. Until then the sensation had been no worse than that of waiting for an overdue meal, but now it became strong, accompanied by a cramp in the stomach, 'a sensation of striction and torsion' as the medical works put it. Otherwise I felt perfectly well, although Jack was rather more affected. He submitted passively to my proposal to make a first medical examination. His tongue was dry and coated and there was a small rash on the back of his hands. His pulse was slow, but still strong and there were no signs of any serious dehydration. He was thirsty but in spite of my advice made no attempt to drink anything. He should have been reassured by my example as I took my regular ration of sea-water in accordance with the figures for safe absorption that I had worked out. We were both constipated, defying the gloomy prophesies of those who insisted we should include a chamber pot in our equipment. Perhaps I may explain this reference. The day we left a so-called specialist in the matter of life-saving at sea had told my wife: 'You will never see your husband again.' When she asked why, he replied, 'Insufficient preparation. They are going to be six weeks at sea and do not even have a chamber pot with them.' If anyone casts doubts on this astonishing conversation, I can produce witnesses.

Thirst did not present a problem for me and was a bearable one for my companion, but for both of us the pains of hunger became worse and worse. We each spoke with longing of the ham roll we had refused just before we left and the thought of it seemed much more tangible and tempting than the most complicated and formal imaginary dinner. It became the one reason for our hunger, the one thing we might have eaten, and I was given a new insight into human desires and regrets.

During the afternoon, when it was my turn to rest, I thought of all the delicious teas we had eaten at the hospitals in Boulogne and Amiens, and every now and again the insidious thought entered my head: 'Why on earth did you leave that comfortable little life and what on earth induced you to get into this scrape?'

Several porpoises were gambolling round us not far away. They seemed quite resigned to our presence and we found their company comforting. What is more, if they could catch fish, there was nothing to prevent us from so doing. It was a clear, calm day and I took a film of them. Unfortunately, all we had to eat was another spoonful of plankton. We could have caught more, but the net acted as a drogue and, near as we still were to the coast, we did not like to spoil chances only just in our favour.

During the afternoon, Jack surrendered to my insistence and began to drink sea-water in small amounts. I had just explained that if he did not make up his mind to do so, his sytem would become so dehydrated that to drink it would be useless and even dangerous. To my great relief, he accepted my reasoning, and the next morning all the incipient signs of dehydration had disappeared.

*c

Even his thirst had gone. We laughed a good deal about his conversion to heresy and our spirits became excellent.

The nights that followed were to bring us a pleasant surprise. We found that very nearly a pint of fresh water condensed in the bottom of the boat. The atmosphere was very humid, and the quantity of the deposit by no means negligible. The dinghy had yet to ship a drop of sea-water and we managed to collect our windfall with a sponge. It was not enough for our total needs but it was a great help. Above all it was fresh water and tasted like nectar.

Towards evening the wind became exasperating. During the day it had been completely unpredictable, both as to force and direction; flat calm would be succeeded by a stiff breeze coming from all points of the compass and the sea became quite rough. Nevertheless, the dinghy behaved very well in spite of the Mediterranean's varying moods. I was rapidly becoming confirmed in my conviction that the dinghy was the ideal form of lifeboat.

We had not seen the coast all day. We knew it was not far away, but it was hidden in a thick heat haze. Jack had been unable to take our position with the sextant and we were not sure where we were. About six o'clock in the evening the coast reappeared, but we could not make out whether we were off Estérel and St Raphaël, or still near Cap d'Antibes. Before we could make up our minds, the sun set for the second time in the voyage and the lighthouses started to send out their reassuring messages. We were between St Raphaël and Cap Camarat, still fairly well out to sea, but not yet quite safe. We were really very hungry and faced the night with somewhat subdued optimism. For some reason or other there seemed to be a light breeze off the sea. Was our expedition going to end by being driven ashore on Cap Camarat, as the 'specialists' had predicted? There seemed little we could do about it, so I went to sleep.

When Jack woke me up at one in the morning to begin my watch I saw that we had already passed Cap Camarat to starboard. At least we were not going to end up there, and if we could get past the island of Levant, the worst part of the French coast would be behind us.

I shall not soon forget 27th May. The sun rose on a splendid day, and during the course of it our chief anxiety was dispelled. In the middle of the afternoon, I was dozing with the fishing line tied round my ankle. (I soon learnt that this was a stupid trick, as if a sufficiently large fish had taken the bait, it might have severed my foot.) Suddenly there was a violent jerk on the line. We had caught a splendid sea perch, or grouper, and we pulled it in with feverish haste, rather, I imagine, as one draws the first bucket of water in an oasis after crossing the desert. What a piece of luck! The creature was carefully gutted and cut into neat slices. We had not forgotten our civilized manners. The head half was kept for the next day and we shared the tail half. The pink flesh almost made me vomit, and Jack obviously felt the same, although I had already tried the effect in the laboratory. It was up to me to show an example. Of course it is delicious, I said to myself, and swallowed the first mouthful. It was by no means so bad and the taboo was broken. Forgetting our careful upbringing, we tore at the flesh with our teeth, each mouthful seeming more appetizing. The rest of the fish was placed on top of the tent to dry in the sun, after we had extracted the juice with my fruit press. At the next meal it almost tasted cooked.

Each civilization has placed a taboo on certain forms of food. Would you eat locusts or white grubs? No. But a Moslem cannot eat pork. Once, in Britain, I even ate whale, but unfortunately I knew it was whale and thought very little of it. Plenty of people will eat horse or cat, if they are told it is beef or rabbit. It is all a question of habit, and I am sure our grandmothers would never have ventured to eat a steak tartare. But I ate so much that day that I was very nearly seasick.

The wind continued warm but feeble, but our full stomachs had raised our spirits again. When a naval patrol boat hove in sight, presumably out of Toulon, we awaited its arrival with calm and assurance. The captain grinned and offered us a few bottles of fresh beer, and although we declined it stoically, we learnt something of the trials of Tantalus. I do not know that this has been reported anywhere, but there would certainly have been a storm of comment if we had accepted it. The incident with the Sidi Ferruch, the ship we met ten days later, was sufficient proof.

After this luxurious, but largely immobile, day, a favourable wind blew up just as the sun was setting, and the lights of the land gradually disappeared in the night. Soon the French coast was out of sight. Contrary to all predictions, we had not been thrown up on it.

CHAPTER V

ON THE HIGH SEAS

∽ ∽ ∽ ∽ ∽ ∽ ∽ ∽ ∽ ∽ ∽

I WAS surprised to discover what incurable landlubbers we were, and the degree of comfort we both took from the continued sight of the land. We saw it disappear slowly on the morning of the 27th with distinct qualms. Our compass course was 210°, that is to say 30° west of south, although with a magnetic declination (or variation) of about 10° west, our true course was nearer south-south-west. This meant that we were keeping an equal distance from Corsica and Sardinia to the east and the Balearic Islands to the west. Before leaving, I had made a study of the prevailing currents and I was expecting one of them, the not very well-defined Balearic Current, to carry us in a westerly direction.

By now we had eaten the last piece of sea perch and were going to have to fast again, although after having caught one, there seemed absolutely no reason why we should not catch more. For the time being it was back to plankton and sea-water, to which Jack was now perfectly resigned, so that drink presented no problem.

On the 29th two cargo boats, one Greek and the other British (the Dego), passed quite close and greeted us. This was exceptional, as both previously and from then on most of the ships we met ignored us completely. Whether this was deliberate or because they did not see us I cannot say, but I became increasingly convinced that it is up to the castaway to look for help rather than to rely on automatic assistance. In our case the lack of recognition was even more baffling, as ships had been advised of our expedition without food and water. I can only conclude that our low position in the water made us almost impossible to see. Shipwrecked survivors must suffer from the same disability, and it is up to them to draw attention to themselves.

The wind freshened and veered during the evening and was heading us straight for the Balearic Islands, but we were getting terribly hungry again and had not caught another thing. It seemed as if there were no fish out to sea and we began to think of it as a watery desert. As night fell, I took the first watch. At first everything seemed normal, but with my senses sharpened by hunger, I started hearing strange noises at about eleven o'clock. Was I the victim of some hallucination? I was a little frightened but tried to reason things out. It was certainly no noise made by man, from whom we were now cut off except for the thoughts of our friends. The noises came from the sea around us, but it was pitch dark and impossible to see anything. I pictured dolphins and porpoises dancing a sort of saraband, doubtless in honour of our frail craft as it pursued its course. The volume of sound was so great, so compelling and lasted so long that astonishment and curiosity kept me awake until dawn, when it became possible to discern huge grey phantoms with a metallic iridescence, all round L'Hérétique.

'Whales!' I cried out, jerking Jack's sleeve violently. We counted at least ten, performing a stately and peaceable minuet round the boat. They must have been between sixty and a hundred feet long. Sometimes one of their number, swimming towards the boat, dived a few yards away, and we could still see his tail on one side when his head was well clear the other. These huge beasts seemed quiet, docile and full of good intentions as far as we were concerned. Jack was rather more perturbed at their presence than I was and was afraid that some brusque movement on their part might upset the dinghy. He recalled the adventure of the brothers Smith, both asleep in their yacht with the tiller lashed, who had roused a whale to fury by colliding with it and been capsized by the terrible blows of its flukes. The whales made off as day broke, but Jack promised that in future he would share my watch if necessary, as he did not share my confidence in the goodwill of our nocturnal visitors. I was delighted and did not hestitate to avail myself of his offer whenever the long hours on watch became too depressing.

Nothing of consequence happened on the 30th, nor did we add anything to the larder. We were slowly getting used to our abnormal existence, and the chief question remaining was how the dinghy would behave in a storm. Would she ride it out again successfully, as her smaller sister had between Boulogne and Folkestone? I believed she would, but Jack was not so sure, although he was prepared to accept the risk. In any case, it would be better to make the experiment in a stretch of sea as busy as the Mediterranean rather than fifteen hundred miles from the nearest coast.

Towards the evening we saw, to our joy, the outline of Mount Toro, the highest peak in Minorca, outlined against the setting sun. It was seventy-two hours since we had left the French coast. Jack had predicted our landfall at midday, when, in spite of great difficulties, he had succeeded in determining our position by taking a sight of the sun at noon. This was an operation incomprehensible to me even in normal conditions, and in those in which we found ourselves it seemed more like a magician's trick. Jack had to coincide in his sextant the lower rim of the sun with the line of the horizon, not always easy to do from the bridge of a ship and a miraculous performance when seated on an inflatable pontoon, bouncing over the waves.

'Land! Minorca!' we shouted. We knew for the first time the almost painful joy of the castaway when he catches his first sight of the land towards which he is steering. Even for us it was high time, as we had eaten nothing but a few spoonfuls of plankton during the last two days, and were racked by hunger. Our troubles, however, were by no means at an end. The coast we had sighted, which looked so near, was to take another twelve days to reach; twice as long as the period we had already spent at sea. If we had known this, I think we would have given up in despair, but instead we began making lighthearted plans for our return to life on shore; we had already worked out the wording of the telegrams we were going to send, and licked our lips at the thought of our first meal in some little inn. Then, all of a sudden, the wind dropped and the sail started to shiver. We scanned the sky, which was slowly becoming overcast with clouds from the south-east, where a storm was clearly brewing. We put out the sea anchor quickly, as we were not yet experienced enough to leave such precautions until the last moment. Hauling down the sail, we covered in the dinghy completely and settled down to wait for the storm to pass. It is worth mentioning, in passing, that its very existence was afterwards denied by the meteorological service at Monaco. Their reasoning was quite simple: their weather charts gave no indication of a storm, therefore there cannot have been one. But the Air Atlas pilots, whose route took them through it, told me that they had thought of us during this period of bad weather.

The squall soon arrived. We were cramped into a narrow space, knees bent, thoroughly uncomfortable, but at least safe. We could feel the waves breaking against the bow of L'Hérétique and the water running over our heads across the tent. It was rather like being in a giant ferris wheel, making great swooping movements while remaining on a horizontal plane. L'Hérétique stuck to the water like a limpet and I felt quite certain that nothing would ever affect its basic stability. It was even possible to write up the log book. All our equipment remained firmly in place, while outside the waves redoubled their fury.

We hardly spoke, apart from occasional exclamations. Crouched under the tent in the cramped sleeping space, we looked at each other fatalistically. Everything was diffused with the yellow light that came through the canvas. Jack looked yellow, I looked yellow, the air itself acquired a daffodil tinge, as we sat helpless amidst nature's turbulence. During this passive and exasperating interlude we tried to guess where we were being driven by the storm. Jack covered sheets of paper with calculations of our possible drift and finally decided that we were being thrown back into the Gulf of Valencia. Picking up the Pilot Book, I learned that this was a dangerous area with frequent storms, usually blowing in the direction of the Gulf of Lions to the north. It was a stretch of sea we had tried to avoid at all costs, but our intentions were not binding on the unmanageable cockle-shell to which we had trusted ourselves. We committed our fate to Providence and tried to profit from the period of inaction by recuperating our strength.

In the semi-darkness of the tent our heated imaginations were prey to all sorts of fears. What would become of us in this fierce battle between the sea and the sky, in which we were tossed to and fro like a sheaf of straw? We counted the hours in the hope that daylight would enable us to feel like human beings again, instead of inanimate things at the mercy of the elements.

The last day of May brought little relief, but although we were gradually being carried away from our destination, there was no further danger, and 1st June rose on a rough and confused sea and a thick fog that you could have cut with a knife. It was impossible to see the bow of the boat. As the day wore on, the fog lifted enough for us to see a large passenger liner pass about a hundred yards away, bound for Barcelona. The wind had settled in the east-north-east and we were still in danger of being driven on to the Spanish coast. We were so weak by now that we had to take turns about three times to pull into the dinghy the twenty-five yards of fishing line dangling uselessly in the water. At noon Jack tried to take our position, although the pale sun was barely discernible through the low fog bank. This proved impossible, and instead he tried to calculate our drift. By his reckoning, we had been carried into the Gulf of Valencia and must be somewhere in the neighbourhood of a little group of islands called the Columbretes, a few miles off the port itself. The day was going to seem even longer and more depressing because of our enforced inactivity.

Suddenly a strange distant noise made us aware that something peculiar was going on. We slid out of our shelter, ready for any eventuality, only to become transfixed with astonishment. About a hundred yards from L'Hérétique, to port, a strange white mass, intangible yet vast, appeared out of the sea like some prehistoric monster. The apparition slowly came nearer while I feverishly loaded my underwater harpoon gun as a last desperate defence measure. Stupefied, I recognized that the beast, some eighty or a hundred feet long, was an extremely rare albino whale, of a type practically unknown in the Mediterranean.

Not only did we need to prove to ourselves that we had not become light-headed, but we would require some evidence if people were to believe our description. Throwing down my totally inadequate weapon, I seized the cine-camera and recorded the monster's menacing approach. We held our breath, expecting anything to happen. I was fascinated by the beast's red eyes, but Jack watched with increasing terror each flick of its enormous flukes, which could easily have shattered the dinghy at a single blow. I tried to calm our fears by recalling the peaceable school of whales we had recently seen, but this failed to dispel the menace implicit in the slow approach of this solitary and unexpected creature. It dived underneath the dinghy, and then swam round us as if to show off its astonishing snow-white skin. Then it slowly turned away and disappeared into the mist.

Hardly recovered from the shock and still discussing this extraordinary apparition, we cocked our ears to a new danger. It was almost as if the whale had been the precursor of a series of trials designed to break our spirit. Barely an hour after the monster had disappeared we heard the ululation of a siren. We both sat bolt upright. In fact, I had heard a faint sound of the same sort several times already, but so indistinctly that I had thought my hearing was probably playing me tricks and had made no mention of it. It had occurred to me for a moment that perhaps we were not so far from land, but I saw no point in awakening vain hopes in my companion. Now there was no further doubt. The noise, which almost drowned the sound of our voices, could only come from some man-made device and the effort to determine its direction made us slightly hysterical.

Tracing the source of a sound in a fog is terribly difficult. I was convinced that it came from the south-west and Jack was equally sure that it came from the north-west. Completely blind as to our true position, we unfolded the chart of the Mediterranean and, forcing ourselves to be calm, tried to determine which stretch of land we might be near. Our fingers met on the same spot: the Columbretes group of islets, about ten miles south of the position Jack had estimated.

Before we could gather our wits, we were assailed by the threat of imminent disaster: the sudden throb of an engine drowned the noise of the siren and every shadow in the mist became a vessel about to run us down. It seemed that nothing could prevent catastrophe. We both clutched at the first thing handy with which to signal our presence; I picked up a mess tin and hammered on it with the handle of my fish press, while Jack beat another pan with its lid. We worked ourselves up into a frenzy amidst the violent cacophony of engine and siren surrounding us. Then they suddenly cut off, to be followed by an almost palpable silence. We sat for a moment or two petrified and then redoubled the noise of our own makeshift fog signals. As if in answer, both engine and siren thundered out again. I felt I would go mad if this went on much longer. Trying to keep a clear head, I made an effort to determine the direction from which this all-enveloping volume of sound was coming. I counted the minutes – ten whole minutes which seemed the longest of our lives. Then the uproar ceased as suddenly as it had begun, and at the same time we suspended our own frenzied efforts.

At that moment, as if a magic wand had been waved, a sudden breeze dissipated the mist, leaving the horizon clear in every direction. There was nothing, absolutely nothing to be seen. We sat in mute stupefaction. We had not been the victims of a hallucination, of that we were sure, but in our somewhat weakened condition it was quite impossible to find any logical explanation for what we have since called the 'Mystery of Columbretes'. For the time being, we decided to try and forget this extra-ordinary occurrence in case it should give us nightmares; our most immediate need was to recoup our strength. When we returned to the matter again each of us tried to put forward some reasonable hypothesis. The most likely seemed that we had heard a submarine surfacing to recharge its batteries, but submarines do not carry a siren. We have never solved the mystery and it will have to remain one of the inexplicable occurrences which castaways of all time have had to endure.

Another ordeal, purely personal but no less unpleasant, awaited me. During the wild night from the 1st to the 2nd of June I had started to feel sharp, stabbing pains in my jaw, typical of a growing abscess. It soon came to a head, due no doubt to the infection of some small cut. A diet of raw fish had probably retarded its healing, as we had noticed that the slightest scratch took days to close up, and that there was a distinct tendency for it to go septic. If it had happened to Jack, I would not have hesitated to use penicillin, but as I had cast myself in the role of guinea-pig, I felt that this would be too easy a cure and one unlikely to be at the disposal of a real castaway. The pain soon became so unbearable that, after sterilizing my pocket knife in the flame of the oil lamp, I lanced the swelling, dusting the incision with one of the sulfa powders. The agony nearly sent me off my head for a moment and Jack became seriously perturbed, but lasting relief soon came; the treatment had not been so bad after all.

We still seemed to provide an attraction for whales, which added their own noises to another disturbed night. The wind continued to blow in strong gusts and the waves crashed over the dinghy's bow with unabated vigour, but through this endless volume of sound it was possible to hear the snortings and blowings of our giant companions. Emboldened by the night, and our apparent harmlessness, they came uncomfortably close and I began to lose confidence in their benevolent intentions. I was afraid they might underestimate their own length as they dived under the boat and would surface too soon, smashing the dinghy and probably putting an end to the pair of us.

Our riding light attracted all manner of sea life; porpoises and various species of fish jostled in its rays. Then two little green lights rose behind us out of the depths. They looked like the eyes of a cat lit up by the headlights of a car. It was a small ray, which I tried to harpoon without success. It was probably just as well, as the flesh is almost as salty as the sea itself and might have damaged our kidneys. What was more unfortunate was that in moving about the boat I knocked one of the oars into the sea. This was serious, as we had only two and were now unable to row the dinghy. We flashed our torch over the water, but the oar had disappeared. We now had to rely entirely on the wind to beach the boat.

The next day, 2nd June, the sky had cleared but the wind, although it had veered to the south-west, was still very strong. We were being forced inexorably into the much-feared Gulf of Lions, and Jack estimated our drift at about fifty miles a day. We had eaten nothing for five days and our hunger had become almost insupportable, even though its symptoms had changed. We no longer suffered from stomach cramps, but from increasing lassitude, an overwhelming desire to do nothing whatsoever. Photographs we took at the time show us both sunken-cheeked and tired out, with bags under our eyes. My face was swollen out of shape. Neither of us wanted to do anything but sleep.

I was dozing about nine o'clock in the morning when Jack, who was at the tiller, called out:

'Alain, Alain, a fish!'

I jumped up and saw another sea perch idling in our backwash between the points of the floats. He was a big fellow, weighing at least ten pounds, swimming with his snout almost on the steering oar, which he ducked under from time to time to scratch his back like a pig against its pen. Whatever happened we had to catch him. My harpoon gun was loaded ready and in a flash I had it aimed over the stern. The instant it touched the water, the fish, in a moment of fatal curiosity, moved in to see what this new object was. I pressed the trigger and the arrow buried itself five inches in his head, killing him instantly and tingeing the sea with blood. Hoisting our prize on board, we sat there blankly for quite a while, devouring it first with our eyes. This was probably no bad thing, as it enabled our stomachs to adjust themselves again to the idea of food.

Something to drink was our first requirement. As this was a good-sized fish I decided to test the method of dorsal incisions, rather like cutting the bark of a rubber or pine tree. The fresh liquid gave us an almost voluptuous pleasure, but the flesh proved difficult to digest. Most stomachs, after all, would rebel against a diet of raw fish followed by a fast, and then raw fish again. But our morale recovered at a bound. We now had food for two days. The storm was still tossing us about, but the weather was getting warmer and the outlook became distinctly more favourable.

As it happened, the next three days showed little improvement. The wind continued to blow from the wrong direction and we ran out of food again. We had not advanced a single yard towards our destination and on the morning of the fourth day we were faced by another period of fasting. This was almost more than we could bear and it did not seem likely that we would be able to carry on very much longer. The Mediterranean just did not seem to provide the means for survival. Several ships passed with a rumbling of engines, but none of them appeared to see us, or if they did, they made no attempt to alter course. We did not hail them, and for all we knew it would have had no effect. However the time was rapidly approaching when we should have to try.

On the morning of 5th June, the eleventh day of the voyage, the weather calmed down, leaving us exhausted, starving, but still confident and determined to go on in spite of it all. The first problem was to find out where we were. At noon Jack was able to fix our position for the first time in six days. We were one hundred and fifty miles north-north-east of Minorca, and the storm had driven us in a great arc. We were going to have to cross the very course we had held a few days earlier, but with typical Mediterranean moodiness the wind had now died right away. There was not a breath of air.

The sea had become completely calm, a mirror broken from time to time by leaping black objects which left concentric ripples. We were surrounded by tunny fish and porpoises, jumping in every direction; the whole sea was a well-stocked larder and somehow or other we had to get our hands on the food in it. When I think of my efforts that morning I have to smile. I had made up my mind that I would try and harpoon a tunny fish, although only a starving man would try anything so bizarre. Hitting one did not present much difficulty, but my fellow under-water fishermen will appreciate only too well the problem involved in bringing in the catch. I put on my goggles, adjusted the respirator and lowering myself into the water I took the gun from Jack. I did not have to swim far to reach the shoal of tunny fish. 'Brrrm!' The harpoon quivered in one of the fish, but it was he who seemed to have done the catching when he set off dragging me behind him. Fortunately even a nylon line has a breaking-point and it soon parted. I swam back empty-handed to the dinghy and with Jack's help managed with difficulty to climb on board again, having lost only my illusions and a harpoon. It cost a considerable effort to hoist myself over the float and I thanked God for my companion, as I would never have been able to make it alone.

Our fast continued, 4th June, 5th June, 6th June . . . The days grew longer, more monotonous and even more exhausting. A small ration of sea-water was our only drink and the plankton, which disgusted us more every day, was our only food. Every movement became a painful and superhuman effort. Hunger had become starvation and our acute condition became chronic. We were starting to use up our own store of proteins, feeding on our last physical reserves. We did not think about it much, as we were dozing or sleeping three-quarters of the time.

The wind was fickle, but we were making some headway in the right direction. On Friday evening, 6th June, we made up our minds to try out our signalling apparatus. If we succeeded in stopping a boat, it would prove that we could attract its attention in case of distress, and we would also be able to send news to our families. We knew they must be worried to death and we were afraid they might ask for an official search to be made for us, which would have meant the end of the experiment. The Mediterranean was proving a good trial run, as we had hoped, but the question of mere survival was not paramount. In fact, this cannot be said to be a problem in the Mediterranean, where survivors must very quickly be rescued by one of the countless ships which use it. On the other hand, in a vast, lonely ocean like the Atlantic it would become the dominating factor. Now that both crew and equipment had undergone their first test, we were in a hurry to get to Tangier or Gibraltar and start the most important part of the voyage. Jack did not want to delay this until September, as he was convinced that the hurricane season then began in the West Indies. In fact, it finishes in September and hurricanes are unknown between November and March. How he came to make this mistake I have no idea.

With all this in mind, we decided that we would stop the first ship and, if necessary, ask for a few rations. It had never occurred to us to broach our own stock of condensed foods, as these were very difficult to come by and would have to be reserved for a real emergency in the Atlantic. There would have been no point in using them for day-to-day needs and they were only there in case we simply could not hold out any longer. Our general health was still quite good and we had not even discussed the idea of using them, as the experiment would thereby have lost all sense. When at about six o'clock, a vessel hove in sight on the starboard bow, we had already planned how we would try and attract its attention. First of all Jack set off two explosive rockets. The ship gave no sign of having seen them. I then took the heliograph, a device which works on a mirror principle, sending a beam of light into the eye of the observer, and tapped out SOS in morse. Still the ship held on its course. It seemed absolutely impossible that we should not have been sighted, but that is the only explanation, although it is almost beyond belief that no one, not even one of the passengers, should have noticed us. It held firmly on its course and disappeared over the horizon, leaving silence once again to descend on the calm sea. But if humankind was indifferent to our fate, the creatures of the sea did not abandon us.

The evening closed on a strange and unforgettable

sight. Just as the sun was setting, it was reflected in a
thousand dancing pin-points on the sea. As I looked at
this sparkling mirror, I realized with astonishment that
it was made up of hundreds and hundreds of turtles,
their shells, seemingly cemented one to another, forming
a solid crust on the waves. Every now and again a head
would appear out of this mass, darting wicked little
gargoyles' eyes at us. One brusque movement on my part
as I tried to harpoon one of them and the whole mass
disappeared as one, like a sheet of metal oscillating into
the depths. Then night, indifferent to calm and storm
alike, fell and enveloped us.

     ◇   ◇   ◇   ◇   ◇   ◇   ◇   ◇   ◇

Saturday, 7th June. Day broke in torrid heat. Only the
barometer, falling steadily, caused pessimism. Jack was
still asleep. I woke him in a low voice. 'Jack, there is a
boat about two miles away.' He grabbed his rockets and
fired them off, one, two, three. In spite of the explosions
and the shower of sparks which lit up the dawn, the ship
held on its course. It was too early for me to use the
heliograph. What were we to do? Was this ship going
to get away too? Does a castaway have to give up all hope
of being seen? As a last resort we had a smoke bomb,
visible by day, which enveloped us in an orange cloud
as soon as we threw it into the sea. We waited, each
second seeming like an hour, but as the smoke cleared
we saw that the heavy bulk of the ship had turned in our
direction. To our surprise, the liner, called the Sidi Ferruch,
made no attempt to slow down.

Once within hailing distance, the captain shouted from
the bridge: 'Is there something you want?' rather as if we
had stopped him to say, 'No, thank you very much.'
'Please report our position and let us have a few

emergency rations,' we replied. The liner then stopped her engines, circled away and stopped about five hundred yards off.

In spite of my exhaustion I had to use the rudder oar as a scull. We reached the side of the ship and exchanged mild conversation with the passengers and the first officer, who passed us down some food and water. Then the captain, somewhat of a martinet, appeared. 'Come on, come on, we have no time for experiments,' he shouted – a perfect gentleman in other words. Jack frowned, but said nothing. He had not had a smoke for five days and was hoping at least to be offered a cigarette, but he was not going to ask for one. The first officer speeded things up, but no attempt was made to invite us on board. Then off went the Sidi Ferruch with her amiable captain.

We did not know how dearly we were to pay for this meeting or how we were to be reproached for accepting this pitiful little stock of rations. Everyone chose to forget that we had spent ten days out of fourteen without food or fresh water and that on the other four we had only had a raw sea perch and fish juice. The mere fact of accepting this minimum assistance branded us as impostors, although our experiences had not differed so greatly from the survivors of La Méduse. We had held out for a whole fortnight, and in spite of their wine and water, most of the survivors of La Méduse were dead when they were picked up on the twelfth day.

CHAPTER VI

CAPSIZE

∿ ∿ ∿ ∿ ∿ ∿ ∿ ∿ ∿ ∿ ∿ ∿ ∿

THE *Sidi Ferruch* steamed rapidly away, and I hope that her captain will never have to make any 'experiments' himself. Little did we realize what a cargo of mocking laughter, calumny and even insult that ship carried off, to rebound on our unlucky heads during the coming months.

Jack gave vent to his fury at the French captain's lack of courtesy and I could only second his remarks. However, our friends and families would be reassured; we had resisted the temptation to transfer on board and our voyage continued. We knew again the exquisite pleasure of drinking fresh water and had a high time exploring the sack of provisions. It contained sea biscuit, four tins of bully beef and one of condensed milk.

The barometer had not lied. In spite of the brilliant sun, the wind had freshened again, but this time from the right direction – it was driving us south-south-west, straight for Minorca. At midday on Sunday, 8th June, the summit of Mount Toro appeared again on the horizon, much more clearly defined than eight days earlier. Were we going to be able to land this time?

The Balearic Archipelago consists of six islands, of which the three largest are Majorca, Minorca and Ibiza. Minorca is the most easterly of them and its capital is Mahon, on the southern part of its east coast, famous for a battle fought there by the Duc de Richelieu, and also

77

for the delicacy we call mayonnaise, originally *mahonnaise*.
We could choose between Mahon and the little port of
Ciudadela on the west coast. It is quite impossible to
land on the north coast, which is composed entirely of
steep cliffs and is the site of many shipwrecks, the best
known being perhaps that of the *Général Chanzy* in 1910.
We therefore had to clear it one way or another.

We steered first for the north-eastern point of the
island, hoping to make Mahon during the night, but the
wind played us false and we drifted further to the west,
finding ourselves not more than a few cable lengths off
the north coast by morning. There was little enough sign
of the flower-bedecked inlets conjured up by the name
Balearics. The coastal resorts are all at the southern end.
For three interminable days we drifted past the cliffs
without any hope of landing. We were extremely close
and I had the cine-camera working overtime. If the wind
blew us off shore again, we would be able to prove we
had been there.

During the course of Monday we drifted slowly
towards the north-western point of the island. We were
so close that I could see a rabbit run across one of the
stretches of green. Hunger was no longer a problem and
I was out fishing underwater every day, bringing in a rich
harvest. During our passage along the coast and during
the whole of our stay, I spent an hour with the harpoon
gun every day, never bringing back less than fifteen
pounds of fish.

We were now in a hurry to make harbour. The Mediterranean voyage seemed to have no great point any more,
and we wanted to be shipped as soon as possible to
Malaga or Tangier or somewhere close to the Straits of
Gibraltar. We would then be in a position to start our
crossing of the Atlantic.

Tuesday, the 10th, found us at sunset a few score yards

off the north-western point. The gentle breeze which had brought us thus far died right down just as we were rounding Cape Minorca. There was not a single bay or inlet in which we could anchor and, to make things worse, the land wind started to carry us out to sea again. It looked as if Minorca was going to disappear below the horizon. Were we really going to start the vicious circle of the Gulf of Valencia again? We tried to stop our drift with the sea anchor, but the current carried us to the north as well, and on the morning of Wednesday, 11th June, the eighteenth day of the voyage, we woke up to see with despair that we were fifteen miles off the coast on which we longed to land.

Then our spirits rose again. A little sea breeze carried us in once more towards Cape Minorca. Once we had rounded it, we knew that Ciudadela was only about a mile to the south. At ten o'clock, to cheer us up still further, we saw a dozen fishing smacks coming up the coast and then dispersing in all directions. None of them seemed to notice us, but one of them went to lift its lobster pots to our north-east. It could not fail to meet us on the way back and we intended to ask for a tow into the harbour. In the meantime we had not been sighted, and we had to concentrate on rounding the cape. Just as we thought we had made it the wind abandoned us again. It looked as though we would have to go through the whole weary round once more, but fortunately a fishing boat came up to us, passed us a tow, and in less than ten minutes, as if in a dream, we made our entry into the little port which, in a matter of minutes, was to adopt and seduce us. The attractions were to prove dangerous for my companion, who, although a model of courage, endurance and even temperament at sea, was unable to resist the temptations of the shore.

Our arrival soon attracted most of the population.

Waiting for us on the mole was a Spanish officer, with an extremely intelligent face, no longer young. As soon as we clambered ashore he came up to me, supported as I was on my shaky legs by some friendly spectators, and said:

'Are you French?'

'Yes.'

'Where are you from?'

'From France.'

'With that?' he said, looking at L'Hérétique.

'Yes.'

'From which port?'

'Monte Carlo.'

'Sir, do you expect me to believe that . . .'

I gave him a newspaper cutting with an account of our intended departure.

Then, looking at our little flag, this splendid old officer took a step back, saluted, and said:

'Eh bien, Messieurs, vive la France!'

Deeply touched, I asked him to note that the seals on our emergency food stocks were unbroken.

It was all a glorious contrast to the preceding forty-eight hours. Our first task was to send off telegrams to our families. Then we each drank a huge glass of iced beer, which tasted like the nectar of the Gods and was served in a little café whose proprietress took a maternal interest in us during the whole of our stay. It felt like being transported to fairyland. Our first guides became our firm friends and showed us all the treasures and charms of their little town. Guillermo is one I still think of, who took us into homes with wonderful souvenirs of Moorish, French, British and Spanish conquerors, with magnificent Queen Anne furniture, Spanish coats of arms and superb Flemish manuscripts. On the first day he said to me, 'This house is yours,' a phrase which, in a man of his race, means what it says. Then there was Augustin, who introduced me to typical Minorcan dishes, particularly *Sobrasada*, which is still such a delicious memory; and Fernando and Garcia who showed me the little inlets where sea perch, mullet and bass gave back confidence to a fisherman too long unsuccessful.

Even my love of music was catered for. Guillermo took me on the following Sunday to meet a Minorcan composer, who had staying with him the superb Majorcan pianist, Mas Porcel, a pupil of Alfred Cortot, who filled my head again with the wonders of Bach, de Falla, Schumann and Debussy. Never has it been so difficult for me to leave any place.

However, the next day, assisted by our fishermen friends, and encouraged by *Ayudante Militar de Marina* Manuel Despujol, the officer who had received us so charmingly on our arrival, we left this enchanting little port amidst the applause of its inhabitants. A sardine boat towed us about five miles out to sea in the direction of Alcudia.

The operation was now becoming familiar. After about half an hour the tow was dropped and we were alone again. This time we did not have far to go: our next destination was Majorca, about forty miles away, and with luck we should be there in the early hours of the next morning. The chief problem was to avoid being carried to the north, no easy matter, as our lee-boards, indifferently mounted and used without much skill, were of little use and the wind was blowing from the south-east. Nevertheless, everything went well, and on the morning of Tuesday, the 17th, we found ourselves right on course. We passed several sardine boats which greeted us in a friendly fashion and we reaccustomed ourselves very quickly to life on board L'Hérétique, in spite of our spell on land. We had taken some food with

D

us, as there seemed no point in adhering to our spartan
régime during such a short passage and we wanted to
keep the emergency stocks intact for the Atlantic. At
about six o'clock Minorca disappeared below the horizon
to the east and the majestic peaks of Majorca stood out
against the setting sun. Everything was going splendidly,
and we soon picked up the lights of Alcudia at a distance
of about five miles.

Jack, who was at the tiller, broke the silence. In his
usual calm fashion he said: 'Alain, we are drifting to the
north, and quickly at that. The wind has veered due
south. I don't like it at all; these north and south winds
cause bad storms in the straits here. However, we'll try
and make it.'

The rocky escarpments of Majorca slid away from us.
Was it back to the Gulf of Valencia again? There was only
one solution, the sea anchor. What an infuriating sea, we
thought, would we never get out of it and into a region
of regular winds? I swore that I would never sail the
Mediterranean again without an auxiliary motor. We
were faced by another night of inactivity, with no idea of
what the morrow might bring. We were getting heartily
sick of the Mediterranean. We were both up at crack of
dawn on the 18th, looking round apprehensively to find
out where we were. The wind had dropped, but we saw
with despair that we were in about the same position as
we had been on Tuesday the 10th, at the same time, but
perhaps a little further out: twenty miles to the north-east
of the north-western point of . . . Minorca. Rounding
the cape, crossing the straits – we had to go through the
whole thing again.

To crown our misfortunes, the wind sprang up from
the north and rapidly freshened to gale force. In the open
sea, out of reach of the coasts, we would have had
nothing to worry about, but with rocks and cliffs in the

offing it was extremely dangerous. There was only one thing to do — make for Ciudadela and wait for the weather to calm down. There was no time to waste, the wind had become very strong, but in about four hours we were close to land again. The sea was very rough and it was clearly impossible to round the fatal cape. As we were turning east to look for some sort of shelter, we met a fishing boat which passed us a tow. Conditions were by no means good; with each wave the tow slackened and then tightened again with a violent twang.

It was not so bad heading into the waves, but Jack did not hide his disquiet. 'Sometimes we have to turn beam on to round the point,' he said. He spoke not a moment too soon. The tow tightened just as we were on the crest of a wave, which then broke on us. In a flash L'Hérétique had turned turtle and we were in the water. I was swimming strongly when I heard Jack, 'The rope, Alain, the rope!' I looked round for a length of line to throw him, although in some surprise, because he was a good swimmer. Then he explained, 'There's a rope round my legs. I can't swim.' Fortunately the fishing boat had come round and took us aboard. While I was still half in the water I shouted, 'Jack, we are going on, aren't we?' And he replied, with true British calm, 'Of course.' What a splendid fellow he was! At sea there was no one to beat him. It was a pity that now and again we had to stop somewhere.

L'Hérétique looked like a tortoise turned over on its back. Every now and again various objects floated out of the tent which still retained them. Braving the danger which increased every minute, of being blown on to the coast, the Spanish fishermen circled round the 'wreck'. Every time something floated to the surface, I dived in to rescue as much as possible. First of all came the sail, then the watertight bags (heaven be praised, the exposed films were saved), then came more reels of film, the rudder oars, the sleeping bags . . . gone for good were the camera and cine-camera, the radio set, the compass and the binoculars. The mast was broken and the tent torn. We entered Ciudadela with L'Hérétique in tow and our tails between our legs.

What had happened? We had been towed too fast in a position neither our sail nor our sea anchor allowed us to take up. The combination of wind, direction of tow and a maliciously breaking wave had been sufficient to capsize the dinghy. We had learnt one lesson for all time: never to drift, even with a favourable wind, without streaming the sea anchor and taking the waves on the bow. But our lives were saved, the boat was intact and our will to go on unaffected; that was the chief thing.

CHAPTER VII

TANGIER INTERLUDE

AS SOON as we had disembarked, I sent off a telegram asking for replacements of the equipment we had lost. The reply was soon back: 'Jean Ferré on way to Palma.' This meant that Jean was probably already there, so we could relax for a day or two while we awaited his arrival in Ciudadela. On Thursday morning I set off early for a long day's under-water fishing.

I was swimming around with Fernando, the local champion at this sport, when a small boy arrived with a message that two Frenchmen had arrived with news of my wife, and were asking for me. 'That must be Jean; he has made good time,' I thought. Mounting a borrowed bicycle, I pedalled for three miles under the torrid sun, only to find when I got to the port that the two men were strangers who had got hold of Jack's log book and were copying it out in the most impudent fashion. I made an effort to be polite to them and tried to give them a full account of our experiences. They already knew most of the details, having questioned the harbour master and read through the log book. They interrogated me the whole morning and then followed me to the house of friends who had invited Jack and myself to lunch, where they took photographs of us without so much as by-your-leave. I learnt that they did not even know Ginette's address, but they seemed in no way abashed and finally took off for Palma, leaving us all open-mouthed. We decided there and then that we would never put ourselves out again.

On Friday morning the same thing happened. Two more Frenchmen arrived and demanded to see us. We went into hiding, only to be discovered an hour later by Jean Ferré and Sanchez, the French Consul at Mahon, both breathless, sweating and furious, convinced that we must have had a touch of the sun and should be locked up out of harm's way.

The news they brought was bad. The expedition's sponsor declined to help us any further and those newspapers which had never taken us seriously had announced, after our meeting with the *Sidi Ferruch*, that the Bombard expedition had failed. We had to get to the bottom of it. Leaving Jack in Minorca, I decided to go to Paris *via* Majorca. After receiving every help from M. de Fréminville, the French Consul, I left on Monday, 23rd June. It was a hair-raising journey. I picked up a car in Valencia at eight o'clock in the morning, was in Madrid by twelve-thirty, at San Sebastian by seven in the evening, and in Poitiers at six o'clock the next morning. Something of a record in itself.

In Paris the battle started. All I wanted was enough new equipment to make us ready for sea again, but no one took us seriously any more. The air was thick with rumours of other expeditions. Someone was going to try paddling from San Sebastian to Dublin in a canoe, and another enthusiast had thought up the idea of crossing the Channel in a 'pedallo' boat. Jack and I were lumped together in the same category. We were laughed at by everyone, and the people who had built the dinghy, even though they had not completely lost confidence, hesitated to assist us further. Our patron, subdued by 'specialists', who contended that they had been right all the time, refused to put up another penny, under the pretext of not wishing to be an accessory to my 'suicide'. I could not make him realize that all he was doing was to diminish our margin of security, as we intended to go on in any case. What had gone wrong? Why was everyone trying to stop the expedition?

It was no easy thing to track down. It was clear that a certain number of people had expected us to be driven on to the Italian coast in a few days, and now that there was a reasonable possibility of our success, they were getting worried. For my part, I was not out to prove the efficacy of certain life-saving equipment, but in particular to show that however insufficient such equipment might be, the castaway still had a chance of saving his skin. Certain parties started to interest themselves in the affair, but I could only guess at their influence until our arrival in Tangier, when it became fully apparent. The whole expedition was in danger, although after long drawn out discussions I did manage to get a few spares. I left for Palma de Majorca, exhausted and demoralized, on Sunday, 29th June. Jack was to load L'Hérétique on board the ship Ciudadela and join me there, so that we could then start off again in an attempt to get as near as possible to the Straits of Gibraltar. If we were held up for any reason, we would, if necessary, take ship as far as Tangier. Once there, people could think what they liked, but it would be difficult to stop us embarking on our Atlantic adventure. My chief fear was that means would be found to have my sailing licence cancelled, which really would mean the end of the expedition. I did not so much mind the idea of people saying, 'He has not been able to carry out his experiment,' but I guessed they would put it another way: 'There must be something wrong with his theories or he would have been able to prove them by now.' I really think it was fear of this second argument which gave me the determination to carry on.

Our spares arrived by plane: a mast, two lee-boards, a compass and a few handbooks. They caused us endless trouble with the Customs, and without the help of M. de Fréminville I think we would still be arguing. Finally, they were brought along to the yacht club, which generously offered us hospitality, and by the next Sunday morning all was ready. Jack had decided to leave late at night in order to take advantage of the land wind to carry us out into the bay. For once we had made up our minds to leave harbour under our own power. Our departure was much more informal than the first from Monaco. Jack and I were at the oars, although a small launch from the club kept us company for a little way. A breeze sprang up from the east. It was goodbye to Majorca. We were on our way again, bound for Africa or the Spanish coast, depending on the wind.

This lap was a pleasure cruise. On the Monday morning, not far off the island, I caught some big mullet and the food supply was assured. It was a magnificent day, the wind driving us along in splendid fashion and Jack had high hopes of making Alicante on the south-east coast of Spain, whence we intended to hug the coast as far as Malaga. But whatever happened we had decided that if the wind should drop we would take advantage of the first opportunity to ship L'Hérétique and ourselves to Tangier. The sooner we passed the Columns of Hercules and reached the Atlantic, the better. The Mediterranean was beginning to give us claustrophobia and we needed the broad ocean to ensure the success of the expedition.

The weather was getting distinctly hot. I swam every day, but Jack preferred to remain in the boat. During the evening Majorca slowly disappeared from sight and we set course to pass as far as possible to the south of Ibiza. On Tuesday morning we could see its coast on the starboard bow. The wind continued favourable and underwater fishing provided us with a positive feast of fish, while schools of porpoises paid us frequent visits. At about four o'clock we realized with some anxiety that we were making very little headway in spite of the favourable wind. A contrary current was holding us back.

If the wind had turned foul, we would have been thrown back to Majorca, so we decided to make for land and beach L'Hérétique at the first convenient place. We got out the oars again, but it was hard work and we were not offshore until nearly nightfall. The sea was studded with rocks and reefs, but with the last gleams of daylight we found an enchanting little bay of crystal clear water and pulled L'Hérétique ashore. We were about fifteen miles from the capital of the island, but it was a warm, starlit night and we looked forward with pleasure to sleeping out, with steady earth under us. We had now given up all idea of beating further round the Mediterranean and had made up our minds to take the first available ship.

A charming farmer invited us to drink some wine with him. It was acid and proved a powerful purgative, but his company was unique. He was completely ignorant of what was going on in the world and had never even heard of Truman, Stalin or Eisenhower. We could hardly believe that such a thoroughly self-sufficient person still existed in the world. Stretched out on our couch of pine needles under the stars, it seemed as if we were on another planet.

The next morning Jack asked me to catch some more fish. I dived in and was back almost immediately with a handsome bass. We spent the whole of Thursday and

*D

Friday in idyllic inactivity, surrounded by high red cliffs and exploring a sea bed as multicoloured as a coral atoll, scintillating with the reflection of hundreds of fish catching the sun's rays. It came almost as a disappointment on the Saturday when, at six o'clock in the morning, the wind sprang up from a direction which should take us to the port of Ibiza. As we rowed out it seemed almost a sacrilege to break the mirror-like surface of the lovely little bay, to leave such a haven of peace for the fury of the open sea. Once out of its shelter, we had to pull on the oars a good bit harder, as the wind had died down again, and by midday it had veered in the wrong direction and we had to seek shelter again in the little bay of Es Cana, near an islet called Tagomango.

We were developing quite a taste for these unscheduled calls and with his usual insouciance Jack was starting to ask why we ever needed to put to sea again. On the evening of 12th July we were accosted by two civil guards, one of whom caressed his rifle and said:

'You are forbidden to land except at a port. You must put to sea again immediately.'

'We can't, the wind is wrong,' I replied.

'That is nothing to do with us,' he said, red with anger.

'Very well, gentlemen, come out with us, you will see.'

That struck home, and these two representatives of the universal police mind found nothing more to say. After consultation with their headquarters, they gave us permission to wait for a favourable wind.

The next morning I was looking for our lunch, when my submarine horizon was transformed by the sight of a magnificent pair of legs. They belonged to Manuela, the eldest of three Chilean sisters, and the swim ended by our becoming five and lunching off a huge water melon.

Manuela had brought with her a copy of Mallarmé which I leafed through. These lines caught my eye:

> . . . I will start! Steamer balancing your masts,
> Heave anchor to reach a nature exotic!
> Ennui, devastated by my cruel hopes,
> Still believes in the handkerchief's final adieu!
> And perhaps the masts, inviting tempests,
> Are those which a wind bends over shipwrecks
> Lost, without masts, without masts or fertile isle . . .
> But oh my heart listen to the sailors' songs![1]

The weather was changing again and the tops of the trees were leaning towards the west. The wind had returned, so we left, and the same day entered the harbour of Ibiza, where the yacht club received us with typical Spanish hospitality. Our Mediterranean voyage was nearly over. On the Friday we embarked on the Ciudad de Ibiza which took us as far as Alicante and there, by emptying our pockets, we just managed to pay our fares as deck passengers, without food, on the Monte Biscargui to Ceuta. Regarded at first with some suspicion, we were marvellously treated by the crew, and the passengers promised to take me to a concert, if ever I should pass through Bilbao. The first engineer showed us round all the ports of call and we made great friends with the radio operator, who nevertheless confided to us in his cups one day that he considered us in poco locos – a little crazy. The captain offered me a replacement for my tattered shirt and the radio operator gave Jack a pair of shoes. One of the stewards saw to it that we did not go hungry.

This, I think, would be a good place in which to sum up the first part of our experiment.

First of all the problem of drink. From 25th to 28th

[1] From The Poems of Mallarmé, translated by Roger Fry; Vision Press.

May we drank sea-water: for four days in my case, and three in Jack's. During this period, our urine was perfectly normal and we had no sensation of thirst, but it should be remembered that it is essential not to wait for dehydration before drinking sea-water. We always found that a good remedy for any feeling of thirst, especially when our faces were in the sun, was to cover them with a towel or piece of cloth soaked in sea-water. Two days on sea perch then provided us with food and drink, but care had to be taken not to compensate too quickly for our fast. Six more days of sea-water followed, bringing us to the safety limit, and then two more days of fish, without any internal complications. In other words, out of fourteen days we drank fish juice for four and sea-water for ten. By interrupting the consumption of sea-water we were able to double what I considered the safety limit.

Food. The symptoms of hunger were these: cramp-like pains extending to the shoulders during the first and part of the second day. On the third day these pains ceased and were followed by somnolence and a permanent sensation of fatigue. To reduce the need for food it is essential to induce an effect of physical hibernation by leading a vegetative existence. Our blood pressure hardly varied, but in this respect I do not think the experiment lasted long enough for concrete results. There was considerable danger of ophthalmia and conjunctivitis due to the reflection of the sun on the sea.

I noticed none of the effects normally associated with the consumption of sea-water and neither Jack nor I vomited or had diarrhoea. On the contrary, we were subject to persistent constipation, without pain, coating of the tongue or mucous membranes or bad breath, and this lasted twelve days. However, we both suffered continuously from wind. We had no lipothymy (fainting spells), and although our skins were dry from the third day onwards there was no sign of petechia (red patches on the skin). There was no oedema of the ankles, although for two days my face swelled up, as is shown in the film I took. Cuts were slow to heal and had a distinct tendency to turn septic.

On the fifth day, I developed an abscess of the first lower molar on the right side, which developed in the usual way. After it had passed, it left a hardening and generalized pain. There was slight drying of the mucous membranes, especially the lips, but only at the start.

I do not propose to enter here into further details, but I would like to say a few words about my equipment and my companion. The dinghy did all that I expected of it; in spite of heavy seas it proved completely seaworthy at all times. Only two items needed strengthening: the mast and the housing of the lee-boards.

Jack was the perfect crew. In sailing from Monaco to the Spanish coast he was responsible for a *tour de force* which many people with knowledge of the sea considered impossible. Most of them expected us to turn up in Corsica or Sicily. As a companion he was active, brave and unselfish. He always chose the uncomfortable jobs and places for himself and was always ready to cope with emergencies. He never complained and never seemed more pessimistic than the situation appeared to warrant. He proved that it was possible to determine a position from a completely rudimentary craft, never lost confidence and was the ideal companion for such an adventure. Jack Palmer would have remained with me and even been the driving force if only I had foreseen that too long an interval on land would lead to his discouragement and final defection. He brought me as far as Tangier, the stepping stone for my great Atlantic adventure. Without him I would never have got there.

When we reached Ceuta, on a public holiday, no one was
at work, and the captain refused to go on and drop us in
the bay of Tangier, declining to listen to our arguments.
In the end, the radio operator intervened on our behalf
and the captain agreed to take us on to Tangier providing
we obtained triple authorization from the police,
customs and port authorities. It was ten-thirty in the
morning and the ship was due to leave at three o'clock
in the afternoon. As we went ashore we heard the captain
guffawing: 'Well, they won't get that. Three passes from
three different offices on a holiday – they won't be
bothering me again!'

By twelve-thirty we had got them all. In response to
our verbal requests the Spanish authorities carried out all
the formalities, and the harbour master had an order
entered in the log of the *Monte Biscargui* for us to be
dropped off Tangier. In fact, we did not leave until nine
o'clock, but about half an hour later, with L'*Hérétique*
ready inflated on deck, we were hoisted over the side by
a crane. The captain had considerable doubts about our
fate, telling us that he would have thought twice about
launching one of the ship's boats; there was a high wind,
such as always churns up the water of the Straits into
choppy waves and flying spume. The *Monte Biscargui* gave
us a last salute on her siren and we were left in the dark
to make for the lights of the international city. There I
was to find many true and generous friends, but also
redoubtable enemies, who were to separate me from my
companion.

We arrived in Tangier at midnight and found our way
through the murk to the yacht club. At long last our
Mediterranean journey was over. Tangier is a large and
handsome town where national prejudices have long
since lost all significance. When I called at the French
Consulate the next morning to pick up my mail, M.

Bergère, the vice-consul, helped me to get a plane ticket to Paris, payable on arrival, and then M. Mougenot advanced me the money to pay for it. The people at the Consulate were also good enough to lend me enough money to buy a decent suit of clothes and book in at an hotel. On Monday, 28th July, I left for Paris, which was, alas, a fatal error on my part, as far as Jack was concerned, for the delay was to lead to a severing of our association. But if we were to make the Atlantic crossing, it had become essential to replace L'Hérétique. There was no point in embarking on such an expedition without having everything possible in our favour. Not only had our inflatable dinghy carried us more than a thousand miles in the Mediterranean, but it had been in service for three years before that. I knew our patron had ordered a twin and I was determined to have the use of it.

I got to Paris the same day, only to find the atmosphere even more frigid than during my previous visit. No one was prepared to put up another penny. In a long session with our patron I gave him an account of our initial findings and enumerated all the reasons why it was essential to continue. At the end of our interview he opened his arms to me and said; 'Whether you go on without me or not, I will help you all I can.'

He gave orders that the new boat was to be delivered to me. The expedition was to continue after all. We agreed to dine together, but in the meantime something went wrong. He had changed his mind again – I was never able to discover why – and now he refused to let me have the boat. Moreover, he did everything in his power to dissuade us from going on. As a concession, I managed to get him to agree to accompany me back to Tangier, where I was sure Jack would be able to convince him.

Before we left we had several conversations with

experts and engineers, whose interest in our preliminary results ought to have been sufficient persuasion in itself. But as far as I could make out, our sponsor was now much more interested in discovering whether it would be possible for castaways to use a patent vaporizer or a battery-driven distilling apparatus. There was even a motor worked by a piece of cord which ran round the boat. As all I wanted to do was to prove that it was possible to live at sea without food or patent appliances of any sort, it became more and more evident that we no longer shared the same ideal. In the end I got the new dinghy direct from the makers myself and flew back to Tangier with it. Our patron was with me, and on our arrival we had a long conversation with Jack. The pair of us had to listen to a long disquisition based on the official theory that an inflatable dinghy would never hold together longer than ten days at sea. We were the wrong people to tell that to, and Jack became very angry. This seemed to be the turning point, and I thought our patron had come round again. He suggested buying us a radio receiver, so that we would always know the exact time at which to take our position.

'They are pretty expensive,' I told him.

'How much?'

'Here in Tangier, about fifty or sixty pounds.'

'And in France?'

'About twice as much.'

'I'll buy you one.'

We went to the dealer, our patron paid the bill and had it made out to Doctor Bombard, Museum of Oceanography, Monaco. The next day he left . . . taking the radio with him.

PART THREE
ATLANTIC

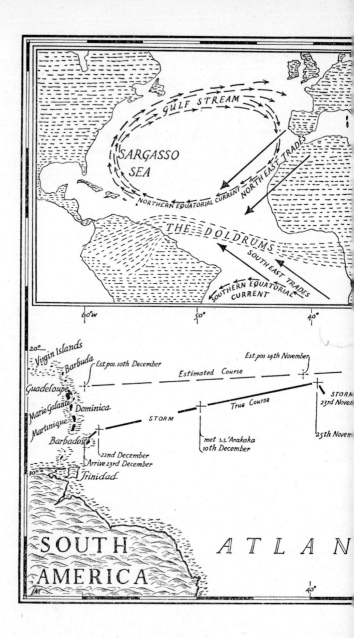

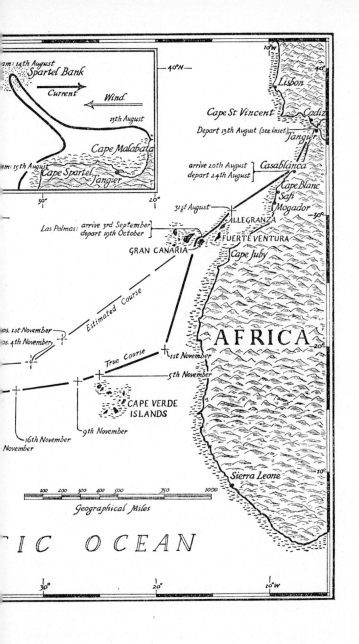

Spartel Bank
am: 14th August

Current →   ← Wind

13th August

Cape Malabata

am: 15th August
Cape Spartel
Tangier

30°   20°

40°N

10°W

40°
Lisbon

Cape St Vincent   Cadiz

Depart 13th August (see inset)
Tangier

arrive 20th August
depart 24th August   Casablanca

Cape Blanc
Safi
Mogador

31st August   30°
ALLEGRANZA

Las Palmas: arrive 3rd September
depart 19th October   FUERTE VENTURA

GRAN CANARIA   Cape Juby

Estimated Course

AFRICA

os. 1st November
os. 4th November   20°

True Course   1st November

5th November

16th November
November

9th November   CAPE VERDE
ISLANDS

10°

Sierra Leone

100 200 300 400 500   750   1000
Geographical Miles

IC   OCEAN

30°   20°   10°W

CHAPTER VIII

LONE VOYAGER

◇ ◇ ◇ ◇ ◇ ◇ ◇ ◇ ◇ ◇ ◇

IT WAS at this stage that I began to notice a change in Jack. His enthusiasm was ebbing little by little, and I learnt some time later that he had told one of our friends: 'If Alain keeps us here much longer, I shall never be able to leave . . .'

In the meantime, offers of help continued to arrive. M. Clemens made us a present of fishing tackle; the swimming club received us in princely fashion; Mougenot contacted one of General Leclerc's old radio operators, named Le Guen, to get us a wireless set; M. Tarpin, a stationer, gave us a pair of binoculars; and M. Bergère helped us out in a number of ways.

In spite of all this active assistance, the wait became interminable. Jack always found a new reason for putting off our departure; either the wind, the tide or the weather. He was the navigator and I had to conform. But one day a taxi driver told me what everyone in Tangier seemed to know, apart from myself. Jack had made up his mind to prevent me from continuing and was convinced that I would never attempt it alone. Terribly disheartened for a moment, I was on the verge of giving up. But then I thought what people would say: 'You see, there is nothing in it, the whole theory is nonsense.' I knew it was not nonsense and I was going to prove it: I would go on.

Brought to the point, Jack finally agreed, but he was now without any enthusiasm. First of all, he suggested that we should stay in the Mediterranean, but I insisted on our original plan. The American Naval Attaché, with whom we discussed the matter, waved a handful of pilot charts and announced firmly that we would never get as far as Casablanca, much less the Canaries. These pilot charts are specially edited by the British and American Navies, brought up to date every two or three years, and give full information about the prevailing winds and currents – although outside certain clearly defined areas the information is subject to local fluctuations. I had spent a year studying the ocean currents and I insisted that what we were trying to do was feasible. It was not too late in the year and I was convinced that over the next month we stood the best chance of success.

After objecting again to the state of the tide, the winds and the lack of charts, Jack agreed, with rather bad grace, to make a start on Monday, 11th August. Knowing that he was by no means convinced, I started to worry; all he had to do was to alter course while I was asleep and I would wake up again in the Mediterranean. If we were going to have to spend our time watching each other, we might just as well give up the idea of setting off. However, the wind had become favourable, and was likely to hold for about three days. Here was an admirable opportunity to pass the Straits of Gibraltar and defeat the current which flows constantly into the Mediterranean. We were towed out by a Spanish ship, but imagine my anxiety when, instead of giving orders to make for the west and the Atlantic, Jack told them to set course for Cape Malabata. This was off to the east, towards the Mediterranean, but he argued that we needed to seek shelter until the wind had died down a little.

The sea was certainly quite rough, but if we did not take advantage of the favourable wind we would never be able to pass the narrows. Somehow the Straits had become a symbol. I knew we had to force this passage, to leave the Mediterranean behind and venture out into the Atlantic: the great ocean's challenge had become an obsession with me.

The Spanish ship carried us steadily eastwards, and we finally stopped off a little beach, almost underneath a house belonging to a friend named Count Ferreto Ferreti. We spent the whole of Tuesday in idleness. On Wednesday morning, the wind was still in our favour, but Jack set off for Tangier at about nine o'clock to make a few last-minute purchases, with the intention of returning as soon as possible. It was the last day we could expect a favourable wind, and it meant that we had to leave by six o'clock in the evening at the latest. When the time came there was still no sign of Jack. I was strung up to breaking point, feeling that if I hesitated all would be lost.

I scribbled a note for Jack: 'I am taking the responsibility of leaving alone. Success can only come if we believe in it. If I fail, then it will be the fault of a non-specialist. Au revoir, old boy. Alain.' This I gave to a customs officer named Jean Stodel, and then, with his help, put out to sea, borne along by a combination of anger, ambition and confidence.

My first task was to pass the Straits and gain as much sea-room as possible in order to pick up the Canaries Current. I was frightened of the coastal rocks, and being so inexperienced, I tried to keep as far out to sea as possible. I was so absorbed in my fight to break into a new world that I was hardly aware of my loneliness; for when one passes from the Mediterranean to the Atlantic, it is not just a question of rounding a point: a difference of a few miles involves entering another dimension and another age. Even the terms of reference change. Time must be counted in weeks instead of days and distances in hundreds of miles instead of tens. Moreover, in order to gain this world, I and my little boat had to undergo an almost impossible ordeal, like some story from the Arabian Nights. Anyone who has seen a river burst its banks or the sea pour through broken dykes, with the great flood of water sweeping away everything in its path, will have an idea of the strength of the really tremendous current against which I had to fight. When the great salmon of northern waters struggle against waters of this force, they are driven by the superhuman, tireless strength which comes of their love and mating. To drive me through the Straits I had my love of adventure, my burning desire to reach the open sea and the call of the ocean which thrust itself at me, as if to deny me any possibility of success. Happily, I had another ally to help me force this barrier: the east wind. But this wind could only be counted on for limited periods. Wind against current, that was the contest in which I had to become the master.

That first night I did not dare take a wink of sleep, because the slightest inattention on my part would have found me driven back into the Mediterranean. The wind blew strong the whole night as I skated over the surface of the current. There was certainly no lack of light, with all the ships criss-crossing around me. I gradually lost Cape Spartel from view and when I glimpsed it again through the morning mist to the south-east, it seemed that I was well past it.

During the morning, while the wind appeared to have blown itself out, the current seemed to redouble its efforts. I tried to get across it. Though I made distance to the south, the land still seemed to be sliding away to my right. I was absolutely exhausted, but I knew I had to complete the passage or give up altogether. I was convinced there must be some way of breaking through. Cape Spartel loomed larger and larger, but when I glanced

at the compass I saw to my horror that the point of the
Cape was to the south-west. It was no good. I was right
back in the Straits. The Gibraltar Current, full of minia-
ture whirlpools, was buffeting my little craft. In my
despair I remembered from canoe trips as a child that it
is always easier to make headway against a current
nearer the shore. The mass of Cape Spartel grew larger
and larger. Then I caught my breath. It seemed as if a
large white villa directly on my beam was falling slightly
behind. After a few agonizing minutes hope became
certainty. I was slowly creeping past the Cape, and,
amidst the splendour of the setting sun, on that memor-
able Thursday, I entered the promised ocean. A small
counter-current, an off-shoot of the great hostile flood in
the centre of the Straits, had come to my rescue and seen
me to the rendezvous with my great adventure.

Now that I was beyond all doubt in the Atlantic, the
first attack of loneliness replaced the hours of tension. I
recognized the enemy at once. It does not come in a
sudden attack, but I was to become very familiar with its
insidious creeping effect during the long Atlantic days.
While I was still near the coast, I knew I could hold it
at bay. Its full effect would only come when I was on the
high seas. At this stage I had many immediate problems
to attend to, which helped me to keep my mind off the
loneliness; but I knew that once the lesser problems were
solved, the big problem would be waiting for me.

The first thing I had to decide was where I was going.
Should it be Casablanca or the Canaries? On the face of it,
the better alternative was Casablanca every time, but I had
to take into account the reactions my solitary departure
might have caused. There might well be people who
considered me a dangerous lunatic whose boat and
equipment should be confiscated in his own interests at
the first landfall. It occurred to me that I might be well

advised to touch nowhere, but I quickly dismissed the idea, remembering that my wife and friends would be in a ferment of worry when they knew that I was alone. Then a much more dubious thought entered my mind: 'After all, if they do stop me, it won't be my fault!' It was a dangerously comforting thought, and I dared not let it develop, but I realized that my subconscious fears were at work.

For the immediate future, I had to avoid being blown ashore on the nearest coast, the eventuality which most of the 'experts' would be expecting, now that I was alone. With a wind from the north-north-east, I was able to set a course roughly west-south-west. If I could hold it, I would be able to follow the chord of the coastal arc between Tangier and Casablanca.

The next thing to master was the art of navigation. I knew how to sail and I could read the compass, so I only needed to learn to use the Cras ruler to determine my course. After a few tentative experiments, I found I could make it work. The principle was simple enough. All that was necessary was to place its point on the next meridian or parallel to the south, and then read the resultant figure, which gave the theoretical course. Then it was a question of adding the declination according to a table, which gave the true course.

I spent the whole of Friday, the 15th, familiarizing myself with the use of this instrument. I saw very few ships. Fortunately the fishing lines with which M. Clemens had supplied me were proving extremely efficient, so at least I had plenty to eat and drink. The catch consisted chiefly of ray's bream (the Brama Raii). I thought of Jack and what a shame it was he was no longer

with me. He had become discouraged at the very moment
when the expedition had acquired interest and purpose.
Now I was a real castaway. I began to keep a daily record
of my blood pressure and pulse.

The following day, Saturday, the 16th, a ship altered
course to hail me. It was a big trawler out of Algeciras,
and the crew was duly astonished at the quantity of fish
I had been able to catch. Fishing was proving a useful
pastime and helped me to forget the vagaries of the wind,
which was proving exasperating: it sprang up regularly
about midday from the right direction and died down
with equal regularity about eight o'clock in the evening.
In the meantime, I started to work at the sextant. There
seemed no great difficulty in measuring the height of the
sun at midday: all I had to do was to adjust the instrument until the lower edge of the sun coincided with the
horizon in the eyepiece. The scale then gave the angle
between the sun, the observer and the horizon, but that
was only the beginning. From this reading I somehow
had to calculate my latitude.

With a little experience, I soon learnt how to do this
with the help of navigation tables I had with me. I did
not need to know the exact time, all that was necessary
was to read off the angle when the sun had reached the
summit of its trajectory. At least it was enough for the
time being, as I was sailing more or less straight down
the same meridian of longitude (Tangier lies roughly
8° 15′ west, and Casablanca 9° 50′ west, a difference of
just over a degree of longitude, which I could afford to
ignore), and I was therefore able to disregard this factor.

Every day I checked the readings the sextant had given
me by comparing them with points on the coast I could
identify on my chart, and this enabled me to confirm my
calculations, or rather, as far as the first few days were
concerned, to invalidate them. At midday, by rare good

fortune, the sea was usually perfectly calm, and the line of the horizon showed clear and steady.

During Saturday I saw several aircraft on the regular Casablanca run and they helped to reassure me that I was on course. Even so I felt terribly alone. I began to debate in all seriousness whether I ought to continue or give up when I got to Casablanca. To be quite honest, an access of fear, or at least a rising state of anxiety, began to get the better of me. As long as I was within easy reach of the coast, nothing much could happen, but after that? Every time I looked towards the broad Atlantic I was appalled by its immensity. Its expanse simply bore no relation to the sea I had just left.

And yet, by Sunday, 17th August, I was brimful of confidence, simply because I happened to have a good laugh in the early morning. It was still barely light when I woke up and then, like a flash of lightning far off in the sky, I thought I saw a flying saucer! I grabbed my camera to film it, only to realize my mistake. It was the planet Jupiter, which a roll of the boat had suddenly endowed with movement. I found the whole episode terribly funny, and confidence returned with my good humour. It only needs the smallest things to change one's mood. Over the course of the months to come my morale came to depend more and more on the quick caprice of minor pleasures and disappointments.

The day soon relapsed into its habitual monotony; a few ships passed, every now and then a plane. I caught no sight of the coast, but at least I knew it was there, and this certainly buoyed up my confidence. During the evening three lighthouses sent their friendly message of identification. I took two of them to be Medehia and Port Lyautey. I crept into my sleeping bag in an optimistic frame of mind.

I slept well every night with my rudder and sail lashed

in position, waking up two or three times a night, just long enough to glance at the compass and sail, see if there were any lights on the coast, and assure myself that all was well. Then I would sink back to sleep amidst a calm which there was not enough breeze to disturb. It was as if the wind hesitated to interrupt my slumbers. But the morning of Monday, the 18th, brought a disagreeable surprise, when I found myself enveloped in a thick sea-mist. At least it taught me the value of the compass.

With nothing else to do, I tried to learn something about astro-navigation, in order to be able to determine my position without depending exclusively on the midday sun. Unfortunately my handbook was in English, and its authors seemed intent on explaining why certain things should be done instead of describing how to do them. I got thoroughly confused, but not unduly depressed. Nevertheless, the sound of foghorns echoing through the mist started to get on my nerves. It was no longer just one, as in the incident at Columbretes, but an incessant chain of noise and echo. They sounded for all the world like some weird race of animals calling and answering each other, and their voices made me feel my utter loneliness more poignantly than ever before. I began to think back on the presence, the point of reference, the sort of ever-present lifebelt, which my companion had represented. If only he would agree to team up with me again at Casablanca or in the Canaries! Amidst the loneliness everything seemed unreal and mocking and I wanted desperately to have someone there who would confirm my impressions or, better still, argue about them. There in the fog, I began to feel that a mirage would appear substantial and that I would be incapable of differentiating between the false and the true. I began to think of only one thing: stopping at Casablanca and not moving another yard. My need for human company was over-whelming. Although the mist was lifting, I could see no sign of land and could distinguish no lights. I was absolutely alone, the land was hidden and the lights seemed to be out. I was just about to become completely discouraged when a tanker emerged from the mist and passed quite close. I hailed:

'Casablanca?'

'Keep on the same course. Bon voyage,' they called back.

I spent most of Tuesday in a rage, which served to keep up my spirits. The days were still made up of eight hours of wind and sixteen of calm, and it seemed as if I would never pick up the trade winds. The number of aircraft appeared to increase, still confirming my course. I was getting near, of that there was no doubt. If only the wind would hold I expected to make Casablanca that evening or the next morning. I worked out a whole series of sums in an attempt to decide how long I was going to need to get from the Canaries to the West Indies. As far as I could make out, it was going to take fifty or sixty days. My morale started to rise. I was still catching any amount of fish and one big ray's bream fell right on top of me. In order to get out of my wake it had jumped and had the bad luck to go the wrong way. I began to brood on how splendid it would taste fried.

At two-thirty in the afternoon I caught the reflection of the sun from the Fedala reservoirs, and made a note in my log: 'Fresh water this evening or tomorrow.'

At eight-thirty I was a hundred yards from the Casa-blanca mole. I had missed the entrance to the harbour and the swell prevented me from seeing the navigation buoys. I decided to spend the night outside. The sound of waves breaking on the mole was not exactly reassuring, but I had quite a good night's sleep. It is much easier to sleep on the high seas than near the coast. For sailors, the land is much more dangerous than the sea.

On Wednesday, the 20th, there was a flat calm, so when I woke up I got out the oars and rowed vigorously to the yacht club basin, where my arrival created a sensation. I was shown the morning paper which carried a banner headline: 'L'Hérétique lost in the Gulf of Cadiz.' Perhaps I had been luckier than I thought. M. Auradoux, the special commissioner, arranged everything with the police and Customs (no easy matter for someone returned from the grave) and Dr Furnestin, head of the Moroccan Fishery Board, presented me with a net for catching plankton. I shall have more to say later about the wonderful reception I received in Casablanca, but in spite of it I made up my mind that nothing would prevent me leaving on the following Sunday, the 24th, at ten o'clock in the morning.

CHAPTER IX

CASABLANCA – LAS PALMAS

‍～ ～ ～ ～ ～ ～ ～ ～ ～ ～ ～ ～ ～ ～

THE WHOLE purpose of the expedition came under discussion again. Two men in particular, who had gone into every aspect of the project and interrogated me on every point, ended up by saying, 'Go ahead, you're all right.' They were Furnestin and a mining engineer, Pierre Elisague. We were surrounded by new friends, all listening, uneasy and anxious, but expressing no opinion and making no attempt to influence my decision. But three men were against the whole thing and tried to discourage me by pontificating about the dangers ahead: the club president, the lifeboat coxwain and the owner of the launch which was supposed to tow me out to sea again. I was alone in the lounge of the club, when I heard two journalists talking.

'We might as well leave; he's not going to start,' one of them said.

'What do you mean?' I interrupted. 'I am only waiting for this fog to disperse to start my tow.'

'You are not going to get a tow,' they replied.

The president had posted a notice that the owner of any launch which towed me out would have to surrender her club burgee, which was equivalent to expulsion.

I went along to see the president and told him:

'I do not want to cause trouble, but I am going to find a tow. If I drown, you will be able to say that you opposed my departure.'

Putting down the charts and instruments I was carrying, I stumped off in a rage to find someone who would take me out to sea. Jean-Michel Crolbois, owner of *Maeva*, one of the two yachts in the basin, agreed to do so.

'Would someone go and get my charts?' I asked, turning to the crowd of journalists and others who surrounded me.

Off they went, and the charts were brought back by Gisèle Vallerey, the swimming champion. This incident the newspapers embroidered with the comment: 'You can see the fellow is a mountebank, he even forgets his charts.'

We hauled out slowly from the port with an escort of launches. I waved to my friends, and we slowly lost sight of each other in the mist. I find these entries in the detailed log I started to keep of my lonely voyage:

'*Sunday 24th.* Cast off tow, off El Hank, flat calm. Mist. Cramp in the stomach, but not hungry in spite of all the tunny fish frolicking round me. Mist thickens and wind drops as night falls, illuminated by precise and impassive winking of El Hank lighthouse.

'*Monday 25th, morning.* Same place, wind freshens from right direction, NNE, but what a mist. Impossible to tell distance from coast.

'*1400 hours.* Coast in sight due south. What can it be?

'*1800 hours.* Think it must be Azemmour. Almost too good to be true. Fish to keep myself occupied. Should see Sidi-Bou-Afi light in fifteen miles. Ought to be to the south-west.

'*2100 hours.* There it is, right where it should be. Fair enough.

'*Tuesday 26th, morning.* Mazagan abeam. Weather very clear. Should be able to round Cape Blanc from the north. If I don't drift I ought to keep steady course of 240 for seven days. Provided I have the courage. Sextant

E

becoming an old friend. Mark the chart. Ought to see Cap Cantin light this evening. That will be last view of land until Canaries.

'Evening. Coast seems to be moving towards me, although my course is parallel to it. As night falls still no sign of Cap Cantin. Light has a range of thirty miles so must still be some way away. Magnificent fishing at dusk, bonito and ray's bream.

'Wednesday 27th. Coast very clear. Wonderful visibility.

'0100 hours. Cantin light to SSW. Hurrah!

'Recognize it all from the coastal elevations in my Pilot Book. Cape Safi in sight. Have logged sixty miles a day, except Sunday. Any amount of splendid fish. Now starting to lose land from view. Must hold course WSW for six days. No weakening. First danger will be that pointed out by Furnestin: risk of passing between Cape Juby and Fuerteventura. Decide to keep as far west as possible. Coast towards Mogador still clearly discernible. Fortunately the Pilot Book describes it as visible far out to sea, which is reassuring. Use of the sextant becoming more complicated, having doubts about this longtitude business. Seem to be drifting to the west, but wind falls again at night. Not exactly helpful to navigation by dead reckoning.'

I find it impossible to reread without a slight retrospective shiver this phrase in my log:

'Thursday 28th. Last brief view of Mogador, then nothing but a blur. Wind very light, seem to be drifting to the west. Full of hope.

'3 o'clock. Wind freshens from NNW. Must watch the drift as I do not want to get too far south. Horribly alone. Nothing in sight. Complete novice as a navigator. Do not know where I am, but only suppose I do. If I miss the Canaries then I am in the South Atlantic, tragic route of the raft La Méduse. Wonderful wind. If only it holds!

'Friday 29th. Wind has kept steady. Have even had to take a reef in the sail.

'9 o'clock. Big cargo boat passes, exactly on inverse course. Must come from the Canaries, so feel I am heading the right way. If only I did not have this problem of how to land. . . .

'Saturday 30th. Lord, what a night! Feel pulped and did not sleep a wink. Squall blew up about 1600 hours yesterday; had to put out sea anchor. It seems impossible: (1) that a vessel as frail as this can weather the battering of the sea; (2) that my heart can hold out. Morale low; really think I shall have to call it off in the Canaries. If only I can get some sleep tonight. Still nagged by this terrible fear of passing between two islands without seeing them, either to left or right.

'Sunday 31st. Drifted further to the south during the night than I expected. Stopped a Portuguese boat at 1500 hours who confirmed my position. Tried to offer me food and water. I refused; from this point of view all is well. Am catching magnificent mackerel every day and am really getting used to raw fish. Atlantic water tastes absolutely delicious compared with that of the Mediterranean. Much less salty and quenches my thirst perfectly. The question is whether things will seem as rosy if this situation lasts several weeks. Course seems good, am 70 miles NNE of Allegranza. If I can keep on the qui vive for thirty-six hours I shall be in the middle of the archipelago. Provided, God help me, I don't sail straight out again. A flock of enchanting little black and white birds comes to keep me company every evening at exactly four o'clock.

'Monday 1st. Have passed one of the worst nights of the whole voyage since Monaco, sea appalling. But I have received due compensation. Yesterday evening, when I turned in, commending myself to the Almighty (I lash the helm and then drop off to sleep), I said to myself: "If my navigation has been correct, I ought to see the first island tomorrow morning on my left," and this morning when I woke I saw, twenty miles off to the south, on my left hand, the two islands with the charming names of Allegranza and Graciosa. What a splendid omen! Now it is up to me not to make a mess of the landing. Full of confidence. I have won the first round and I shall win the second.

'*Tuesday 2nd.* Appalled to see what a distance separates the islands and the terrifying void which will swallow me up if I miss the coast. It is quite impossible for me to retrace my steps, something I shall have to bear in mind. Once I have left the Canaries, or if I miss them, there will be no possibility of return. The minimum distance to cover will be 3,750 miles. Convinced I can make it, but there is still the problem of the acute anxiety I would cause my wife and friends, not to mention the triumph which would be enjoyed by those who predicted I would never reach Las Palmas. If I want to triumph, I must provide the proofs. I said I would arrive at the Grand Canary; I will land there and not drift away. It would have been a relatively simple matter to land on the first islands I sighted, but I must prove I can go where I wish. That is essential for the castaway who, like me, must be able to reach the point he has selected.

'*Afternoon.* My inflatable dinghy, generally considered unsteerable, astonishes me more every day. Every morning about eleven o'clock, I have to deflate it slightly so that the air expanded by the sun does not burst it like a balloon. I blow it up again every evening. Ship practically no water and sleep peacefully. The first few nights were difficult. I woke up with a start every few moments with the sensation that some catastrophe was about to strike, but I have gained confidence. If it does not capsize during the day, why should it do so at night? Cannot possibly sit day and night with my hand on the tiller. Have realized that with the wind from aft, the dinghy will sail straight before it, with or without fixing the rudder, and have learned to trust the steadiness of the wind. Can sleep perfectly soundly away from the land, but what is going to happen when I have to steer for shore? Impossible to sail into the wind; the most I can do is to keep it on the beam.

'Wednesday 3rd. God help me, what is going on? Spent the whole night on the look-out for the Las Palmas light, must be there but cannot see a thing. What on earth am I to do? Ought I to stop and wait for the fog to lift? Or ought I to keep on to the south?

'Noon. The first clue, an aircraft passes to the right; it was still climbing after the take-off; the land must be there, I shall make it after all.

'3 o'clock. It is no good, cannot possibly make the coast. I thought the plane had taken off from the northern part of the island, and now that the coast emerges through the haze I see that I have drifted past twenty-five miles of coast and only have about six left on which to make a landing. Wind from the north, am drifting to the south with a strong current. I shall pass about three miles from land, but I can never reach it.

'6 o'clock. Perhaps after all I have a chance, a counter-current is starting to compensate my drift. The southern point of the island, looking out on the immensity of the South Atlantic, is still to my left. Maybe . . .'

I still had some reason to hope when I wrote those words. At about eight o'clock I was not more than a hundred yards from the beach, but I was so terrified by then that I thought seriously of abandoning the boat and swimming ashore. The chief problem was not to be torn to pieces on the rocks. Some fishermen had caught sight of me and a gathering crowd pointed out a spot where I could beach on sand between two reefs of sharp rocks. I finally made it. It was the first time that a rubber boat had proved it could be steered for nine hours in an unfavourable wind. I had been so paralysed with fright that it was several hours before I could walk properly, but at least I had landed on the island I had named as my destination.

I had proved not only that I knew how to navigate, but that I could make very good time: I had taken exactly eleven days (from 24th August to 3rd September) to get from Casablanca to the Canaries. Gerbault had taken fourteen days for the same crossing, Le Toumelin twelve and Ann Davison twenty-nine.

The navigational problems I had surmounted were these: for the first time in my life I had steered by instruments on the high seas. However, as I had no particular confidence in my sextant readings, I had maintained a parallel set of dead reckoning figures. I made a note each day of the number of miles I estimated I had covered in the direction indicated by the compass. That gave me a theoretical position which took no account of the possibility of drift. I then allowed myself a margin of safety, based on my probable rate of drift, taken from the force and direction of the current given in the Pilot Book. It was a factor which could not be ignored even though there was no physical evidence of its presence. This treacherous force, which was as real as it was intangible, was gradually carrying me to the south and could have resulted in my passing between the islands and the African coast. Every day therefore brought me three possible positions: one that I had calculated, one that I had estimated, and – most pessimistic of all – the possible true position if all the unfavourable elements had played their part to the maximum. Bearing this last point in mind, I had concentrated on avoiding the Atlantic maw always open before me.

'But', it may be asked, 'since you had set off to cross the Atlantic, what would it have mattered if you had missed the islands and carried on with the most important part of the voyage?' A valid question, but there were three good reasons for stopping: first of all the anxiety of my friends and family, who assumed that this lap would only take a fortnight; secondly, the consideration of morale: if I had missed my first target, I would have taken it as a very bad omen. Finally, the thought that if there had been no news of me for a fortnight, the authorities would probably start a search for me. They might or might not have found me, but if they did it would have been the end of the experiment; if they did not, few would have believed in my good faith when I arrived in the West Indies seventy or eighty days after my departure from Casablanca.

◇   ◇   ◇   ◇   ◇   ◇   ◇   ◇   ◇

Eleven days' sailing had brought me again on *terra firma*. The little village of Castillo del Romeral, about ten miles south of Las Palmas, gave me a princely reception. When the dinghy was sighted, the inhabitants came flocking to the beach, convinced that I was a real castaway. I was therefore greeted by a sort of general assembly from the village and surrounding farms, simple, welcoming people, colourfully dressed, all waiting for me on the beach.

The coasts of the Grand Canary are extremely rocky, and although I had succeeded in landing on a small section where sand predominated, there were plenty of sharp outcrops menacing the inflatable dinghy. It only had to move a few feet to the left or right to be punctured. The bystanders soon solved that problem. With its little tricolour flag flying proudly, L'Hérétique, still fully loaded, was lifted on to the shoulders of twenty strong men and carried further inshore. Two more of them helped me to stagger with it. Manuel, the local 'chief', came up and asked the expected question: where had I come from? I gave him the usual answer in my best Spanish:

'De Francia, de Niza, después Baleares, Tanger, Casablanca y once dias de Casablanca aqúi.'[1]

It was clear that this passed his comprehension. He looked round to see if anyone else had heard my incredible statement. 'Aures habent et non audiunt.' I could see that their native politeness to a guest was tinged with a certain scepticism. It took several days to convince them that what I had said was true. Manuel took me to his home, where I was immediately served with a fried egg, and we were joined by the local medical attendant-cum-schoolmaster. In spite of my overwhelming fatigue and sleepiness, I had to spend the whole evening telling my story in a doggerel of iberized French, which my companions somehow managed to understand.

[1]From Nice, France, then the Balearics, Tangier, Casablanca and eleven days from Casablanca to here.

CHAPTER X

TEMPTATIONS
OF TERRA FIRMA

I TRIED to find out how to get to Las Palmas to cable
news of my arrival and make contact with the French and
Spanish authorities. My friends reassured me; a car (with
the charming nickname of the 'Pirate') would be available the next day to take me to the capital. Manuel was
as keen as I was for me to get in touch with the authorities. He wanted to be relieved of this new encumbrance,
or at least regularize the position with the customs and
the police. A month or so earlier a yacht called the *Dandy*,
coming from Finland *via* Casablanca, had been wrecked
on the same part of the coast. With the innocence common to fishermen in every country, those of Castillo del
Romeral had salvaged most of the jetsam, and had seen
nothing wrong in quietly retaining the greater part of it.
Manuel himself had had some difficulties with the coast-
guards and he wanted no repetition of the trouble on my
account.

In the meantime I had to get a night's sleep. The
question was where. In the school? There was no proper
bed, but I stretched out on a table used for first-aid
purposes. There was not much give in it, but no well-
upholstered interior-sprung mattress has given me a
better night. The only trouble was that the earth seemed
to have acquired a peculiar rocking motion, and at one
moment I almost felt seasick.

The next morning, 4th September, the 'Pirate' was there waiting for me. Manuel protested loudly when I made an effort to pay him something. A final wave and I was off.

The island unfolded before me in all its savage splendour. Bare and menacing pinnacles of rock dominated what I took to be old lava beds, on which were perched enchanting little villages. Young girls with fresh faces were out drawing the day's water (its supply is apparently the major problem of these Fortunate Isles). With arched backs and proud bearing, they seemed to walk without effort, carrying on their heads the most diverse vessels, ranging from the classic earthenware jar to the corrugated iron drum.

This part of the coastal plain is covered with banana trees, and I soon became familiar with the green flat-leafed shrubs, condemned to a short life by their growth cycle. Each bush grows for one season, and then has to make way for its successor. One slash from a billhook cuts short its ephemeral existence, leaving the shoot which has grown under its shadow to flourish for another short span. There are very few trees, because of the shortage of water; but the date palms looked particularly attractive, accustomed as I had become to my watery desert.

In due course a twin-towered cathedral in the distance announced the proximity of Las Palmas. I had read about it in my Pilot Book, which described the church, visible from the sea, in such detail, that my guides were convinced that this could not be my first visit.

Las Palmas itself has a magnificent port, the Puerto de la Luz, one of the great harbours of the Atlantic. I went straight to see the harbour master, brother of a well-known heart specialist. He was expecting me. Some journalist friends from Le Petit Marocain had flown over a

few days earlier from Casablanca on the first flight of the
Armagnac, a large cargo plane inaugurating a new service.
They had looked out for me all the way over, and
after seeing no sign of the raft, had made enquiries
about me on arrival. So nearly everyone knew about
my trip.

Before embarking on the next and most vital part of my
journey I asked the harbour master to check my sextant
to avoid any errors in calculation.

'With great pleasure,' he replied.

Certain newspapers reproduced this incident thus: 'He
asked for some lessons in navigation. The harbour master
refused, not wishing to contribute to his suicide.' When
this appeared in print, an engineer wrote to me offering
the necessary instruction, a more practical way of pre-
venting disaster. As I lost his letter, I was unable to thank
him. If he reads these lines I hope he will accept them as
an expression of my gratitude.

While I was still with the harbour master, the French
Consul came to look for me; it was the start of a delightful friendship. M. Farnoux was a second father to me,
putting me up in the Consulate, and introducing me to
the charms of the island although he himself had not
been long in Las Palmas. When I went to his office for
the first time, the most important business man in the
French colony on the island, M. Barchillon, came in to
make my acquaintance. We became an inseparable trio.
M. Barchillon constituted himself our mentor, and with
his help all doors were opened to us. My circle of French
friends was soon increased by the members of the yacht
club. Unlike most such institutions, three-quarters of
its membership consisted of real yachtsmen and only a
quarter of loungers. I cannot possibly name all those who
helped me, but I must mention Collachio, Caliano and
Angelito, who entertained me so charmingly and made

my stay so delightful that it became almost impossible to take the final decision to leave.

I had decided not to return to France, but to stay about a week in the Canaries for minor repairs, putting everything in perfect order, rather than battle at home for additional equipment, even though it might have made things easier. The Consul approved of this decision, but my other friends, Barchillon and, above all, the senior pilot, Angelito, begged me to think things over carefully before setting off.

'I know the sea,' Angelito said. 'What you have already done is magnificent, you have more than proved your case, but believe me, there will be no fish to catch in the middle of the Atlantic.'

Angelito meant well, but he did not realize that his objection was the one most likely to spur me on. If I had stopped then, there would be more than enough people to say on my return: 'You have done very well, but it wouldn't work further out in the Atlantic: off the Continental Shelf there are no fish to catch.'

The second and more important part of my experiment was yet to come. I had already proved that it was possible to survive on raw fish; what I now had to demonstrate was that it was still possible to catch the fish in those parts of the ocean which orthodox minds contended were barren.

The Consul and Barchillon understood the reason for my determination, and went out of their way to help me, the one in his official position, the other with his resources. I was only waiting for a telegram from Ginette saying, '*Au revoir*'. It did not arrive for a day or two and I had time to cruise in a yacht towards Fuerteventura. Still nothing came. Finally, one morning, a telegram arrived at the consulate: 'Happy to announce birth of Nathalie. Our congratulations to L'*Hérétique*.'

My new daughter must have recognized her responsibilities and made an effort to be there for the great day of departure. The temptation to return to France now became too great. I felt I could not possibly set off without seeing her. When I announced in the club my intention of paying a quick visit home, those who, out of friendship, had tried to dissuade me from continuing my trip thought that they had triumphed. Manuel, the old friend from Castillo del Romeral, made a special journey to the Consulate to ask, 'Is it really true that Bombard is giving up?'

Farnoux gave him an evasive answer. At bottom, I believe they all thought, 'He is perfectly sincere when he says he is going to continue, but we can be sure that his wife will now stop him from embarking on this folly.'

Through the good offices of the Consul, a place was booked for me on the direct Las Palmas–Paris plane, and on 12th September I left. When I passed through Casablanca, a crowd of friends was there to greet me at the airport.

There was a further surprise at Orly. Two journalists were waiting for me. Some of the newspapers were already saying that I intended to give up now that my child had been born. But nothing could shake the courage and faithful self-abnegation of my wife. She was confident, had seen me at work, knew that what I was attempting was possible and understood my purpose: to save lives, thousands of lives. Not that she was happy to see me leave, but she saw the necessity for it and knew that I must complete my voyage to prove my case. She made no attempt to restrain me.

Then I was afflicted by the last act of what I have called the Comic Interlude. The day after my arrival, two gendarmes knocked on the house-surgeon's door at Amiens:

'We wish to speak to you in private,' they said to me.

I remained silent.

'This is the point: there is a matter of eight thousand francs in costs to settle. You have not paid them and you will have to come with us to the clerk of the court, or go to prison.'

'For how long?' I asked.

'Twelve days', they said, and showed an order for my arrest.

I just did not have that much time to spare for prison. So I paid up the eight thousand francs, a splendid piece of financial assistance to the expedition.

         ᵒ   ᵒ   ᵒ   ᵒ   ᵒ   ᵒ   ᵒ   ᵒ   ᵒ

Freed at last from vexations, I spent three delightful, mollifying days. However, the newspapers took up again their cry of, 'He will not resume his voyage,' while Palmer went on record in Tangier as saying, 'It would be suicidal madness to set off from the Canaries at this time of year.' The expedition was surrounded by an atmosphere of scepticism. The birth of my daughter was regarded as the decisive factor. In the meantime I pottered around, went to see a sick friend living near Poitiers, and then took the plane back to the Canaries via Casablanca. I wanted to spend a few days studying plankton in the research department of the Moroccan Fishing Board, and to go rather more deeply into the question of the fish I was likely to catch in the waters I was about to cross.

I had also made up my mind to get a wireless receiving set. I had given up the idea of a transmitter, even if one were to be offered to me. My reasoning was this: I would be completely alone on board, because there was now no question of Jack rejoining me and I had no intention of finding a successor. It would therefore have been extremely difficult, if not impossible, to work a generator while I was transmitting. In any case, I was incapable of repairing the smallest defect, and one missed contact would have convinced everybody that I was dead. The strain on my family would have been too great.

On the other hand a receiver would be very useful. Longitude is determined by the difference between solar time at any given point and Greenwich Mean Time. There is a difference of four minutes for each degree of longitude, that is to say an hour every fifteen degrees, and I could carry in my head the jingle: Longitude West, Greenwich Best; Longitude East, Greenwich Least. A radio receiver would mean that I should not be completely dependent on my chronometer. I could check it against radio time every day; but I would need a set able to stand up to the conditions. Unfortunately funds were low.

I would have to trust to luck. Perhaps in Casablanca someone would help me out. But I had hardly anticipated the warmth of my welcome. There were over a hundred people waiting for me at the airport, including an extremely attractive young lady with a bouquet of flowers in the colours of the City of Paris. There was a fine old regular naval officer, an expert in life-saving at sea, who had taken up the cudgels in my defence when someone had said to him, 'It is prayer books he needs, not navigation manuals.' He told me that the newspaper Le Petit Marocain, indignant at my episode with the two gendarmes, had opened a subscription list to pay my fine. The first donation had come from Admiral Sol, Naval Commander-in-Chief in Morocco, and the total was growing fast. At last I was going to be a man without a police record. One might call it the end of the Comic Interlude.

◇   ◇   ◇   ◇   ◇   ◇   ◇   ◇   ◇

I was inundated with invitations, with the Navy well to the fore. My friend Pierrot lent me his flat, the Fishery Board welcomed me with open arms, and I started to look for a radio. At least I suffered no loss of weight. One group of friends who invited me to dinner at eleven o'clock at night were surprised at my lack of appetite. They did not realize that in order not to offend anyone I had already accepted one dinner invitation for seven o'clock, and there is a limit to one's appetite. The problem of the radio was soon solved. My friend Elisague and his *alter ego*, Frayssines, offered me a superb battery set which is still in front of me as I write these lines. They had made for it a completely watertight nylon cover, which even protected the telescopic aerial. They went so far as to present me with certain small rubber articles usually used for another purpose, in which to keep dry the silica salts, which I was to use for de-humidifying its interior.

As a final honour, I received an invitation one morning to visit Admiralty House. I was received by a small, brisk gentleman, dressed in tropical whites, who, with all outward friendliness, subjected me to a searching interrogation. He questioned me about my aims and my means, set me navigational posers and, in other words, extracted every ounce of information. I can only record now what pleasure the Admiral gave me that day. I had been waiting for a long time for someone in authority seriously to seek the truth of what I was about. At the end of this friendly but searching session, the Admiral said to me, 'We understand what you are after and we are going to help you.'

It was thanks largely to this admiral that I had the feeling every time I met a foreign ship, Spanish, British or Dutch, that I was a unit of the French navy. He gave me his own marked Atlantic navigation manual, and he was the only professional sailor to write to me before I left: 'You will succeed.' *Scripta manent*, Admiral, as you knew when you did me the honour of writing a dedication on my chart.

There were, as well, two other sailors who sent me encouraging farewell letters; Jean Merrien, author of *Navigateurs Solitaires*, and Jean Laurent, director of the Laboratory of Hydraulics, who wrote: 'When you have succeeded, which you will . . .'

But the time had come to leave. Casablanca was becoming so attractive that every day increased the wrench of departure. On 5th October I took the plane for the Canaries. We landed at Teneriffe and I was soon back in Las Palmas. There another fortnight was taken up by the efforts of friends, nature, sport and music to detain me.

The music was that of the concerts and the theatre, the friendship that of the yachts' crews I remembered so well, of *Maeva* and *Nymph Errant*, which had arrived during my absence. Such is the marvellous fraternity of the sea that I remember one evening in the *Nymph Errant* when the eleven yachtsmen were made up of nine nationalities: three Englishmen, an American, an Italian, a Spaniard, a Swiss, a Dane, a Dutchman, a Frenchman and an Australian girl.

Nature exerted her charm through excursions to Cruz de Tejeda and Agaete in company with my charming guides, Calmano and Collachio, and the sporting attractions included our sessions at the swimming pool, where the adorable lady champion of Spain gave her dazzling exhibitions, and I was beaten in a two hundred metres crawl by that dynamic elder, M. Boiteux *père*.

'Watch out, Alain, if you stay too long, you will never have the strength to leave.' This thought came to torment me during long, sleepless nights. But there was nothing to be done, the wind was still in the south. Until it veered, there was no point in starting. Perhaps the new moon would bring some improvement. Finally, on 18th October, the wind changed, and I announced that I would leave the next day.

CHAPTER XI

ATLANTIC CHALLENGE

∽ ∽ ∽ ∽ ∽ ∽ ∽ ∽ ∽ ∽ ∽ ∽ ∽ ∽

THAT Sunday, 19th October, the wind finally blew
steadily from the right quarter: the north-north-east. At
long last the trade wind had arrived. A French yacht was
to tow me out of the harbour. My friends rallied round
in a heart-warming fashion, showing a spirit of understanding which touched me deeply. M. Farnoux, our
Consul in Las Palmas, took me to mass in the morning
and then accompanied me to the yacht club. His first
intention had been to join the yacht which was going to
tow me, but we were both becoming quite emotional,
and fearing to upset me even further, he suddenly said
in an almost gruff tone of voice:

'I don't think I'll come after all. Don't be angry with
me.'

As if I could have been! I embraced him and we parted.
It was Boiteux père who finally came with me to L'Hérétique.
My equipment and stores of food, checked and sealed
by the consular authorities, were already on board,
together with the radio set which I had been given.
Angelito, the head pilot, made one last inspection and
gave my sextant a final check. While all this was going on,
quite a crowd had gathered. I was given the club burgee
and asked to sign the golden book. All my friends were
there and even strangers went out of their way to show
their goodwill. I was astonished, once we had set off, to
find myself at the head of a veritable convoy, which

accompanied me out of the harbour mouth with all the
ships in the port sounding their sirens. Sailing yachts of
every shape and size tacked and crossed all round me,
their white sails looking like seagulls; some of their
occupants made the sign of the cross as they passed,
to bring me luck. We all felt that the supreme test was
about to begin.

As if to encourage me on my way, a great three-
masted sailing schooner, the cadet training ship of the
Spanish navy, was hove to where I had decided to cast
off my tow. I felt that fortune, in the guise of this survivor of the days of sail, had contrived this encouraging
gesture. There she lay, lifting gently in the swell, one of
the last reminders of the ghost ships, long voyages
wracked by scurvy, the castaways of La Méduse, of those
who had died of hunger and been engulfed in the man-
eating sea. I had just cast off my tow when I saw the
training ship's flag dip slowly in salute; all the cadets
lined along the rail removed their caps as I passed. The
thought struck me for a moment that in all the world's
navies this was the manner of showing respect to the
dead. To show I knew I would win through, I hoisted
my sail smartly and slowly drew away from the little
yachts still tacking and crossing and saluting either with
their flags or their mainsails.

Gradually they were lost from sight, all except the big
schooner, who then gave me the last and most splendid
salute. The midshipmen furled and then let go their three
topsails in a whipcrack of wind and canvas which echoed
across the water. It sounded more as if they were greeting
my triumph than honouring my departure.

        ◦   ◦   ◦   ◦   ◦   ◦   ◦   ◦   ◦

The evening was completely clear, the wind blew steadily

from the north-north-east and the dinghy forged ahead at a good three and a half knots towards the south of the Grand Canary. I intended to hold a south-south-westerly course before turning due west. My position was exactly on the twenty-eighth degree of latitude north and fifteenth degree of longitude west. My goal in the West Indies lay roughly on the sixtieth degree of longitude west, with several possible landfalls between the twelfth and the eighteenth degree of latitude north. I had decided against setting a westerly course straight away, in order to avoid the Sargasso Sea which, with the Doldrums, was one of the two major dangers of which I had to steer clear.

North of the route I had chosen, the Northern Equatorial Current and the Gulf Stream formed between them a gigantic eddy some five thousand miles in circumference, containing a great mass of seaweed, the origin of which has always been a mystery: this is the Sargasso Sea, a great, dead expanse. It is said that no form of edible fish has ever been caught there. The whole area has always been a major navigational hazard, a terrible trap, where plant filaments and seaweed grip vessels in an unbreakable net. To the north it was the sea that spelt danger. To the south the winds were the menace. Here the two powerful trade winds, one blowing from Portugal in the north-east, the other from the Congo in the south-east, meet in a tremendous conflict in a no man's land of violent storms, unpredictable turbulence and disquieting calms, a sort of buffer state between the northern and southern hemispheres. It is called the Doldrums, a region of anarchic violence of the elements which was very nearly fatal to Mermoz, and from which I knew I would not be able to free myself if I were caught there. To my right I was threatened by the currents, to my left by the winds.

The stiff breeze which had sped me on my way did not last for long; it abandoned me during the evening. Looking at my useless sail, I wondered how long the calm would last, for I had no previous experience to guide me. Slowly and relentlessly the current carried L'Hérétique to the south. I fixed my lantern to the mast so that I would be seen by the numerous ships which cross between the Grand Canary and Fuerteventura. With my steering oar lashed, the tent-cover pulled up to my neck like a blanket, my head on the lifebelts, I dropped off to sleep about half-past eight. L'Hérétique drifted slowly in the dead calm. It was a cool night under a lovely, luminous sky.

The next day, and the day following there was still no wind and I was in exactly the same position as on the day of my arrival when the mist had hidden the islands. I was completely isolated and knew only that there was one island to the right, another to the left, and that I could not see a thing. I was impatient to get out into the broad Atlantic, where I would no longer need to show a light at night – there would be no ships to see me.

Monday had brought the first sign of life in the sea around me. Unfortunately, they were still only small fish which swam ahead of the dinghy like pilots. They were difficult to catch and would have provided me with very little food. I began to fear that the calm would never break, but during the afternoon of the third day, a breeze sprang up and I was able to set course for the twenty-first parallel. I intended to hold this course for about ten days, assuming it would bring me about a hundred miles to the west of the Cape Verde islands, whence I would head straight for the West Indies. That day I wrote in my journal:

'Morale excellent, but sun hot. Very thirsty. Drank a little sea-water as the fish are still sulking; have only been able to catch about three pounds, quite insufficient to provide fresh water. However this should improve. Water seems much less salty than in the Mediterranean.'

That night my situation was really brought home to me. It was all very different from the dummy run I had made across the Mediterranean, a busy, civilized lake, criss-crossed by ships. Now I was in a boundless ocean, with little likelihood of meeting any vessels. The Atlantic would really put my theories to the test. Right from the start, everything combined to bring this realization home to me.

The trade wind sprang up again. Soon it approached gale strength. Carrying me first on their crests and then in their troughs, the waves either protected me from or exposed me to its blast. Their tops were breaking all round me. I wondered what would happen if L'Hérétique came just under one of these on-rushing waterfalls.

Unable to do anything about it, but confident in the dinghy's stability, I dropped off to sleep, expecting an untroubled night. It became a nightmare. Suddenly, half in a dream, I seemed to be surrounded by water. Confused and panic-stricken, I tried to gather my thoughts. Was there still a boat under me? Was I in it or in the water? I started swimming, and then struck out desperately. Half dead with fright I woke right up. L'Hérétique was completely submerged. I realized that a wave must have broken right on top of me. I must start baling at once. Only the inflated floats showed above the water. Everything else had become part of the sea, but L'Hérétique continued imperturbably on its course, like a wreck. Once I had woken up there was no time to be frightened. Almost instinctively I started scooping out water with my two hands and then with my hat, a ludicrous utensil for what seemed a superhuman task. I had to bale furiously between each big wave so that L'Hérétique would survive the next. But even with a proper baler I would have needed to display a degree of energy which would soon have exhausted me. Each big wave hit the stern-board with a thud, and the water flowed in anew, making the work of the previous ten minutes or quarter of an hour useless, pointless and hopeless. It is still beyond my comprehension how, numbed with cold, I managed to keep this up for two hours. That was the time it took to get the dinghy properly afloat again. I can only say to my fellow castaways: be more obstinate than the sea, and you will win.

I was safe, but everything in the dinghy was completely soaked, and when the sun started to dry things out, they would all be covered with a film of salt, which was going to absorb the humidity every time night fell. The whole craft had become a sort of salt marsh. Most of the equipment was in watertight containers, and fortunately the radio had not been affected. The matches, on the other hand, were absolutely soaked. In due course, I spread them out in the boat to dry in the sun, with very little hope of their ever being any use again, but at least I had to try. Fortunately I had about a hundred boxes with me, but I would be lucky to find one in each box that would light.

There was still land in sight, which I assumed was the last I should see. The one great satisfaction I had was that L'Hérétique was at least never going to capsize. The dinghy had behaved exactly as I hoped, like an aquaplane or floating platform, sliding over the crests of the waves without offering any resistance. There was a reasonable hope that she would reach the other side in one piece.

The following night, fearing a similar disaster, I lowered the sail as soon as the wind showed signs of freshening. To prevent being flooded by another breaking wave, I let go the sea anchor, turning the bow to the swell. But it was exasperating to have to sacrifice the night's run. I had yet to catch a single fish, but the concentric wakes they made round me proved that there were plenty there. As I had foreseen, two days would bring me all I needed.

There is no entry in my log for Thursday, 23rd, because I was too busy all day with needle and thread. The wind had blown up fresh and strong from the right direction; the faithful trade wind from the north-east which was to carry me to my destination. But fate has its own ironies; hardly had I trimmed the sail to the wind, when it tore right across at its broadest part. It had brought me all the way from Monaco to the Canaries. When I started off again, I had made up my mind to use it as long as possible, and then replace it with the new sail I had in reserve, but I had not expected I would need to change them so soon. I threw out my sea anchor, lowered the sail and rigged the new one to the yard. Half an hour later a sudden violent gust wrenched it off and sent it flying away like a kite. I saw it splash into the sea a little way off. What was worse, it had carried away not only the rigging, but also the main sheet and halyards.

I had no alternative but to rely on my old, torn sail, so I started laboriously to sew it together again. All I had was a reel of ordinary black thread and a few darning needles. I had to work on it inch by inch, as the lack of space prevented me from laying the sail out. I had to mend the rent little by little, just as I had slowly baled out the boat, and was gradually to win my battle over the elements. By the time evening came, I had just about finished. I was very tired and preferred not to subject my handiwork to too severe a test. After all, it was the last sail I had and I could not afford to have it torn away. I had to put out the sea anchor again and resigned myself to the loss of further precious hours.

During the whole of the rest of the voyage I always had a pang of fear when I looked at the black darn right across the sail, rather like a piece of scar tissue that threatens to burst. But above all I was afraid of the very fear it engendered, because increasing tiredness and exhaustion led me to expect the worst, and this in its turn made me weak and cowardly. From this moment on I was prey to an inner conflict of morale, quite as vital as that with the elements. When things were going badly I managed to cope with it, but when there was some slight improvement I began to fear the worst again. I began to have doubts about the ability of my equipment to last the course. My low spirits that night are perhaps explained by the fact that I was frozen, chattering with cold, soaked to the skin and encrusted with salt. Never had I waited so desperately for the sun to rise, it seemed that it would be my only salvation. I had either forgotten or had never really learnt what a dangerous friend it could be.

I had at this time made very little progress, and, what was worse, had very little idea of exactly what distance I had covered. It was the start of my errors in calculating the longitude, which were to have serious consequences, as I shall note in due course. I was still in the area where the trade winds blew strongly. It was only later, when their effect was distributed over a larger area, that they were to diminish in force. For the time being, the waves were the greater menace, tall and white-capped, like a malicious child showing its pearly teeth. As one does in front of a child, I tried to hide my fears, and hoisted my patched sail.

I had hardly gathered way again when the harvest of fish began. They appeared first as green and blue stains in the water, timid to start with, and approaching the dinghy with great suspicion. They disappeared with a flip of their tails as soon as I made any sudden gesture. However, it was high time to start laying in a supply. During the whole day of the 24th I worked at bending the point of my knife, gently, without breaking it, on the flat part of an oar, as if on an anvil. I then bound the handle of the knife with a length of twine to the end of an oar so that I could harpoon the first fish which came near enough. Almost anything will serve as a lashing – a necktie, shoe laces, a belt or strands of rope; a castaway would always have something of the sort. I intended to dispense as far as possible with my emergency fishing kit (normal equipment, in a sealed box, carried by most life-boats) as someone on a raft might well be without it. I intended to do what I could with the material on board. While I was working away, I was astonished to see several birds, wheeling overhead. I had been convinced there would be none once I was out of range of land, and the sight of them exploded another landlubber's notion. No day was to pass without my seeing some form of bird life. One bird in particular became a personal acquaint-ance. Every day of the voyage, he appeared at about four o'clock, to circle a few times over L'Hérétique. But for the time being I was concentrating on the fish.

On Saturday, 25th, after half-catching and indeed wounding a number of fish and then seeing them wriggle off the end of my makeshift harpoon, I managed to catch my first dolphin (or, to be correct, dorado. This is a fish, not a mammal, but I shall use its more common name). I was saved, not only did I have food and drink, but bait and hook as well. Behind the gill cover, there is a perfect natural bone hook, such as has been found in the tombs of prehistoric men, and which I think I can claim to have adapted to modern use. My first fishing line was at hand. From then on I had all the food and liquid I needed every day, and was never in danger of starving.

That was probably the most heretical aspect of my self-imposed role of castaway.

◇   ◇   ◇   ◇   ◇   ◇   ◇   ◇   ◇

During these first days, I was not yet completely alone on the sea's expanse. A number of large ships passed me, apparently bound for the Canaries, but not one altered course to assist me. I shall never know whether I was actually sighted, but it is more than likely that someone in a raft is very difficult to see. I was to have more than one proof of this. On the other hand, L'Hérétique was surrounded by an absolute shoal of fish, which never abandoned me. Fishermen and experts had prophesied before my departure that once I had left the Canaries I would never catch a thing. Precisely the contrary happened. The green and blue patches I had noticed became the silhouettes of large, familiar fish, jostling round the dinghy. I was to get to know their spiny backs well, recognizing them as old friends. From time to time a crack like a pistol shot attracted my attention, just in time for me to see a silvery underside disappearing into the waves.

The wind had now become predictable and regular. I left my sail set night and day, and with no land obstacles to avoid I was able to run before it without worry, watching the slightly faster swell roll past me. Just as speed assures a cyclist's balance, so it gave me additional security. If I had stopped, the waves would have broken against my stern-board and flooded the boat.

I could not help feeling worried about my equipment, particularly the patched sail, wondering whether it would stay the course. I wrote in my log: 'Before I left, I was convinced that my chief anxiety would be to obtain food and drink, but it transpires that worry about equipment and the no less serious problem of humidity, are worse. I have no option but to continue using the damp clothes I have with me, otherwise the cold would kill me.' And I noted, already at this early stage: 'A castaway should never take off his clothes, even if they are wet.'

I realized, even though I had been soaked to the skin on the second day, that wet clothes succeed in conserving the body's warmth. I was purposely wearing the sort of clothing that a castaway might have, trousers, shirt, a pullover and a jacket. Wiser now from experience, I no longer regarded as figures of fun the mussel and shrimp catchers who always wear the warmest clothing they can get, with long woollen stockings, and stout waterproof boots, in spite of the weight involved when trudging through the shallows.

By Sunday, 26th October, I had written in my log: 'Can no longer determine my longitude with certainty. I shall just have to guess it from the time the sun reaches its meridian.'

This problem had acquired grave importance. In principle, the height of the sun above the horizon at noon should enable me to determine my latitude, and the changing time at which it reached its zenith should give me my longitude. When I left, I was on the fifteenth degree of longitude; I should therefore have found the sun at the summit of its trajectory at one o'clock by my watch which was set to Greenwich Mean Time. In fact, when I first timed it, the sun reached its zenith at twelve-fifteen. I estimated that I needed to make a correction of forty-five minutes, an error which was to lead me into others still greater.

That day I found in my pocket a note from my friend

John Staniland, owner of the yacht *Nymph Errant*, who was due to leave the Canaries three weeks after myself. It gave the address to which he had asked me to telegraph news of my arrival in the West Indies: 'John Staniland, c/o King's Harbour Master, Bridgetown, Barbados, to await arrival of British yacht.' He must have known that he would get there long before me, but clearly wanted to encourage me by suggesting that I would get there first.

I was still over-optimistic. I wrote in my log: 'If I am where I think I am, I should be at latitude $21°$ north by Wednesday, changing course to the west on Thursday, covering 700 miles in ten days. I still have 1,800 miles to go; another 25 days at my present speed. However, I must not be too optimistic.'

The main thing was to be of good heart, and I was full of hope during most of the crossing. It seemed as if I had left only the night before, although I had already been at sea a week. Now that I am back, I am often asked if I was not bored. That at least is something that never happens at sea. This adventure formed a separate compartment in my life. Although each day seemed interminable, time had lost all relative importance. There were no points of reference on which to base its passage, such as appointments, the day's normal rigid time-table. Time passed without my being aware of it. Only later, when this existence had acquired a patina of normality, did time begin to weigh heavily, when I was able to compare a particular day with others exactly like it.

    ⟋   ⟋   ⟋   ⟋   ⟋   ⟋   ⟋   ⟋   ⟋

The second week brought an anniversary which made me a little homesick. It was my birthday. After I arrived in Barbados, and people asked how old I was, I used to reply: 'I was twenty-eight at sea.'

My luck was in that day and offered me a sort of birthday present. My home-made fishing line, the hook baited with a piece of flying fish, was trailing in the wake when a big bird, which in English is called a shearwater, and for which I have yet to find the French name, pounced on the bait. I pulled it slowly inboard, a little worried in case he might peck holes in my inflated rubber floats. No sooner did I have him in the dinghy than he seemed to have an attack of seasickness, vomiting all over the deck. The creature was only half-conscious, and with a slight feeling of repugnance, I wrung its neck.

I had never eaten raw bird-meat in my life, but after all steak tartare is a delicacy, so why not the flesh of a bird? My strong advice to those who catch a sea bird is not to pluck it but to skin it, as the skin is very rich in fat. I cut my shearwater in two, ate one half immediately, and left the other to dry in the sun for the next day. But I was soon disillusioned if I thought my birthday dinner was going to give me any respite from my imposed diet. The flesh was excellent, but it had an undeniable taste of fish.

During the night I received something of a shock. Through my tent I noticed a curious light. At first I thought I had somehow caught fire, but it was only my half of shearwater giving out a strong phosphorescent light, so strong that it was reflected on the sail, giving it quite a ghostly appearance.

The 28th October brought an event which was to have dire consequences, although I did not realize it at the time. I broke the strap of my watch, one of those self-winding models actuated by movements of the wrist. I fixed it to the front of my sweater with a pin, assuming that my movements would keep it going, but in the cramped interior of the dinghy, they were to prove insufficient. It stopped soon afterwards, and it was too late to set it again.[1] It became impossible to determine with any certainty what progress I was making to the west, the direction of the islands where I hoped to land. This incident brought home to me how much the aimlessness of doing what I pleased, of not deciding in advance how to occupy my day, was beginning to weigh upon me. I decided to work out a strict time-table of activity. I am convinced that in such circumstances it is essential for the castaway to remain master of events, rather than be content merely to react to them. In order to get away from the constant and unrelieved proximity of the sea, I decided to adopt the peasants' habit of getting up and going to bed with the sun.

At dawn I collected the flying fish, which cannoned unsuspectingly into the sail during the night and fell on top of the tent. I collected the first on the third day out, and during the rest of the voyage picked up between five and fifteen every morning. I ate the two largest for my breakfast. Then I fished for an hour, catching more than enough food for the day. I divided my haul into two parts, one for lunch and one for dinner. Why did I not change my meal hours, it may be asked, instead of eating at the accepted times of morning, noon and evening? I felt that having already altered so radically the nature of my food, it would only place an additional strain on my stomach to change its working hours. It had acquired the habit of secreting certain gastric juices at certain times in order to digest the food it received, and I saw no point in disrupting its functions further.

After the hour's fishing, I devoted the same amount of time to a minute inspection of the boat; the smallest area of friction could have proved fatal. The back of a book, the deck boards, even the radio, rubbing gently on one

[1]After my watch and, later, my radio, had failed me, the times given in my log were based on guess-work.

spot would have sufficed to wear a hole in the rubber floats in a few days. Those who now visit L'Hérétique in the Naval Museum in Paris will note that despite all my precautions, there is quite a worn surface on the right-hand side, where I used to rest my back.

At the end of forty-eight hours I noticed with a shock that the mere fact of leaning against the inner wall had been sufficient to rub off the paint. I had to find some-thing to put between myself and the float to prevent further friction. Once the paint had gone I would start wearing away the rubberized canvas, rendering it no longer watertight. I put my ear to the floats to check if I could hear any sign of rubbing, rather like a doctor sounding someone's chest cavity with a stethoscope, and carried out this inspection every day. Like a human lung, the air-filled float transmitted and amplified noises. The faintest sound would have enabled me to track down a puncture. I took a further precaution. There was clearly going to be a gradual loss of pressure in each section of the floats, not necessarily identical. At night I therefore closed the valves between the sections, leaving them open during the day. If one of the sections had lost more air than the other there would have been a whistle as air passed through the valve to compensate the pressure when I turned the cock each morning. Thank God this was something that never happened. But the detailed morning inspection, when I ran my fingers over the whole surface, combined with the sounding, several times saved me from catastrophe. Every castaway should regard this tireless vigilance as an imperative necessity.

I then did half an hour's exercises to tone up my muscles and keep myself supple, after which I caught the two coffee spoons or so of plankton I needed to keep scurvy at bay. This took me between ten and twenty minutes. The trouble was that any net trailed from the

F

boat acted as a brake and I had to make up my mind whether to catch just a little plankton and keep up my speed, or gather enough to serve as food and reduce the day's run. I therefore decided that as long as there was plenty of fish I would treat the plankton as a sort of medicine for its vitamin C content.

Noon was the time for taking my position. To make quite sure of getting a good sight, I spent half an hour beforehand practising with the sextant, as the dinghy was always very unsteady. As the sun rose to its zenith, the increase in the angle got smaller and smaller, until it appeared to remain steady. That was the crucial moment. In spite of the great difficulties caused by my lack of elevation over the horizon, I soon became very adept at this little game. The mistake to avoid was that of taking the crest of a wave for the true horizon. The swell was strong but regular, as there was no nearby coast to modify its pattern. It had a rhythm in which every sixth or seventh wave was higher than the others, and its summit gave me a clear view of the horizon. Focusing through the eye-piece of the sextant, I used to count the waves without looking at them, and on the seventh I took the bearing. At that second I had to make the lower rim of the sun coincide with the line of the horizon by adjusting the arm of the sextant so that they appeared in the eye-piece in exact juxtaposition. Although I had been anything up to ten miles out in my calculations at the beginning of the voyage, by the end of a week I was determining my latitude to within a mile or so.

The afternoon was the longest and most difficult part of the day, with no way of hiding from the pitiless sun. I devoted the time to reading, writing and my medical studies. At two o'clock I gave myself a complete physical check-up; blood pressure, temperature, state of the skin, nails and hair, condition of the mucous membranes;

noting the sea and air temperatures, humidity and weather conditions. Then I subjected myself to a sort of examination of my state of mind and morale and tried to exercise my memory, after which I read the books and music scores I had with me and did regular translation work.

When the sun passed behind my sail, giving me some respite from its rays, I carried out my evening medical examination; measurement of urine, muscular strength, stools passed, plus a résumé of the day's activities; the day's haul of fish, its quantity and quality and the use I had made of it, a note of the day's plankton catch, its nature, quantity and taste, and a description of the sea birds I had seen. Dusk brought the night's sleep and I allowed myself the luxury of an hour or two listening to the radio after the evening meal.

During the course of the voyage, one problem became increasingly insistent: to discover the best position to take up when sitting became uncomfortable, which it soon did. Either I used to sit on the floats with my legs hanging down, or on the deck boards, my back resting against one float and my legs on the other. In the first position my legs grew heavy and I ran the risk of oedema of the ankles; and in the second, not only did my raised legs start to ache, but they had to lie across the oars, which bit into them and forced me to change my position continually. Sometimes I stretched out on the planks, but as I was starting to lose weight, my bones began to ache on the hard surface and I could not maintain the position for long. It was practically impossible to stand upright; the best that I could manage was to squat on half-flexed knees, balancing against one of the floats in interminable contemplation of the sea. As an additional security precaution I had fastened a line about twenty-five yards long round my waist, with the end attached to the base of the mast. The dinghy was remarkably stable, but I only had to change position for it to rock and I always needed to hold on to something. Fortunately it neither pitched nor rolled, but just rocked. Nevertheless, I always had the feeling that a single wave could put an end to the whole expedition. All round me, giant waves were breaking with a noise like thunder. Any one of them breaking over the dinghy could have made short shrift of both the experiment and my life.

On 28th October I noted: 'I am not dreaming about food; a good sign.' Indeed, it was the best proof that I was not hungry, because hunger is above all an obsession. I had no cravings of any sort.

The next day I was suddenly overwhelmed by the thought of the grave situation I was in. Apart from its length, this part of my voyage had an inexorable quality absent from the previous laps. It was impossible for me to stop or turn round, there was not the slightest possibility of any help. I was just a drop in the ocean, part of a world not to be measured in human terms. I often had cold shivers down my spine and I had not sighted a ship for some time. The previous day I had seen my first shark since leaving the Canaries, but it passed quickly by. The dolphins, on the other hand, had become familiar acquaintances, I even talked to them at times, as the only friends in sight. When I woke up during the night I was always struck by the beauty of these creatures, swimming parallel to me, and leaving phosphorescent wakes like some shooting star.

From sheer curiosity I thought I would see what effect the beam of an electric torch would have. As soon as I switched it on, all the fish concentrated in its circle of light. I was still lost in admiration of their intricate evolutions, which I could direct more or less at will, when a sudden buffet forced me to clutch the side of the boat.

It was a large shark, the upper part of its tail much longer than the lower. It had turned over on its back to swim towards me. All its teeth flashed in the light of the torch, and its underside gleamed pure white. It butted its snout repeatedly on the side of the dinghy. Whether it was trying to take a good bite I do not know, but I had always heard that sharks turned on their back to seize their prey. I was much alarmed, being not at all accustomed to such rough manners. The only shark I had seen up till then, between Casablanca and the Canaries, had followed me at a respectful distance, but this one had probably lived too far out to sea to learn such civilized behaviour. I snapped out the light in the hope that it would go away. For a moment or two its tail continued to beat around me like the cracks of a whip, splashing me with sea-water from head to foot. Its white stomach appeared from time to time amidst the phosphorescence, but then, presumably bored by my inactivity, it made off. It is more than likely that the attack was serious, but I comforted myself with the thought of how difficult it must be to bite a football. This somewhat reassured me, but I hoped that in future such undesirable guests would keep their distance. I had also learned my lesson and never again flashed my torch on the sea. From that day, encouraged by the complete absence of sea traffic, I also decided to save paraffin by no longer showing a navigation light. My morale was still high, although I was beginning to suffer from the cold at night, the effects of immobility and the consequences of never being dry, due to the humidity. I was beginning to show the first physical effects of my ordeal. I noted in my log book:

'Have lost the nail of the small toe of my right foot, and there is a strange rash probably due to the salt on the backs of my hands. Afraid of getting boils, which I know will be terribly painful, and which I would try not to treat in order to give no false values to the experiment. I have a few antibiotics on board, but if I use them, future castaways may object that they had no medicaments. Have made up my mind only to use them as a last resort.'

I was also experiencing the first general effects of solitude and fatigue, and found myself comparing my situation with a more normal existence: 'Am paying a heavy price for all the pleasant days I have spent on land,' I noted and – still the optimist – I comforted myself by calculating that I only had between twenty-five and forty days to go.

It is amusing (although at the time it was rather pathetic) to see how the route I marked on my chart betrayed my nostalgia for dry land.

'On reaching latitude 21° north, I shall turn right, taking 255° instead of 230°.' Even the figures began to read like highway numbers and I really felt at the time that my next move was to take the first turning to the right. I felt that I should be able to find my way about the limitless ocean as one does about a town, just because I knew where I wanted to get to.

'In writing up the log, I have missed taking my latitude; no matter, I can do it tomorrow, there is plenty of time. After all Columbus took twenty-two days at this time of year for the same voyage; I am expecting to do it in thirty-five or forty. I must learn to vegetate and live the contemplative life; if I think too much the day seems to last longer.'

The next entry asked a question: 'I wonder if things would be easier if I was not alone. I really think so. Why is Jack not here? Well, it is no good thinking about it. My God, this trade wind is strong. As long as the sail holds out, it's all right, I shall get there more quickly, but I am absolutely soaked.'

Thursday, the 30th, was a day of delirious optimism.

The entry reads: 'Another twenty-three days' (which would have meant my arrival on 23rd November); but I did add as a rider: 'providing all goes well'.

This optimism may seem surprising, and sound as though I am inventing it after the event, especially in view of the possible duration of the voyage I had already calculated. But I had always borne in mind the necessity of making a generous allowance to calm the fears of those at home. Had I said that the crossing would take thirty-five days rather than sixty, my family and friends would have started worrying after twenty days, instead of after thirty or perhaps forty.

'A beautiful day and night, calm and without incident. I dreamed about my library of gramophone records. A plane passed right above me, certainly without seeing me. Slightest friction still a serious menace.'

This last remark referred to the tiny inflatable emergency dinghy which I kept in the bow of the boat so that I could blow it up rapidly and launch it in the event of some accident. During the night, one of the guy ropes of the sail had rubbed constantly against it, making a neat little round hole. Only one night of friction by some quite light body was therefore sufficient to puncture the rubberized tissue. It was a very salutary example, although my first reaction was one of severe shock. In the case of any accident to L'Hérétique I no longer had anything to keep me afloat. It is true that my chances of survival in the emergency dinghy would have been extremely small. It was a small, one-man float designed to save people in difficulties near the beach; I can hardly believe it would have got me across the Atlantic. However, the damage deprived me of the pleasure of launching it at the end of a line, so that I could photograph L'Hérétique forging ahead in the middle of the Atlantic under full sail. In fact, circumstances were reducing me more and more to the condition of a real castaway. In my case as well, the craft I was in was my last chance.

'Am counting up the days too often and it only seems to make the time pass more slowly. My catch of fish is diminishing in number, but increasing in weight; can now drink from the fish daily by cutting slits in the flesh. It is no longer necessary to cut them into pieces and use the press. No longer need to keep any pieces in my shirt to dry for further use. What a superb day! Fresh trade wind starting to fall off somewhat; it is now a strong breeze, but still from the right direction. As far as I can make out the latitude is about 21° 28′ north, more or less in the estimated time.'

I was to learn later that the longitude was only about 18° or 19° west. At the time, however, I was convinced that I only had to make another 35° to the west and 4° to the south, that is to say 1,800 or 1,900 miles, and I was sure I had already covered a quarter of my route. My true position will be appreciated in due course. The entry for Friday, 31st October, was as follows:

'Wind freshened a little during the night. Making good speed. A superb shearwater flew over and I tried to catch it, thinking nostalgically of the bird on my birthday. But this one refused to co-operate.'

The previous evening had been splendid and I listened to Schubert's lovely *Seventh Symphony*. Curiously enough, it became almost the signature tune of the voyage, because although it is not played all that often, I heard it six times during the sixty-five days I was at sea.

I was still bursting with optimism, and noted the same day: 'Should sight land at any time after Saturday, 22nd November.' I was, in fact, destined to see it on 23rd December, a whole month later. I already seemed to be having doubts about my navigation as I noted at four o'clock:

'Navigation is by no means a simple affair. There is all this business of declination to be taken into account, but my Atlantic route chart does not give it. The problem is to know what headway I have made to the west; whether the compass course is a true one, or whether the westward variation has altered. If the variation is more westward, then I am on a more southward course than I think. The change in my latitude should have confirmed this, but my true speed is so difficult to measure that it is almost impossible to navigate by dead reckoning. Assume that I am making eighty miles a day [an estimate which was to prove stupidly optimistic], should do better still [even more crazy!]. The most important thing is to remain between the seventeenth and eighteenth degrees of latitude north. Tomorrow, if I am on the right course, I should be on 20° 20' north. The trade wind is marvellous. Longitude is about 26° 40' [that was the real error; I was still, approximately, on the eighteenth degree], which leaves about 33° to go to the west, roughly 1,700 miles, say 22 or 23 days at eighty miles a day.'

Then I added: 'If the wind holds, that must be the pattern of it; surely I must know as much about navigation as Christopher Columbus.' The solitude must have been starting to affect me the day I wrote that. I had begun to understand the difference between solitude and isolation. Moments of isolation in ordinary life can soon be ended; it is just a question of going out of the door into the street or dialling a number on the telephone to hear the voice of a friend. Isolation is merely a matter of isolating oneself, but total solitude is an oppressive thing and slowly wears down its lonely victim. It seemed sometimes as if the immense and absolute solitude of the ocean's expanse was concentrated right on top of me, as if my beating heart was the centre of gravity of a mass which was at the same time nothingness. The day I

*F

dropped the tow off Las Palmas I thought that solitude was something I would be able to master, once I had become accustomed to its presence on board. I had been too presumptuous. It was not something I had carried with me, something that could be measured by the confines of myself or the boat. It was a vast presence which engulfed me. Its spell could not be broken, any more than the horizon could be brought nearer. And if from time to time I talked aloud in order to hear my own voice, I only felt more alone, a hostage to silence.

On 1st November I reached latitude 20° north and *turned right*. My course was now west, still a few degrees to the south, but very little. I had to try and cover the degrees of longitude, and put the dinghy on the opposite tack, that is to say the sail had swung from the right side of the boat to the left and in the normal course should have stayed in that position without being touched until my arrival. In fact, I was no longer steering the boat at all; I had lashed the rudder so that the dinghy followed the compass course.

From time to time, every two hours or so, I checked the course and occasionally made some small adjustment to the rudder position. The night was spent in a constant condition of dampness, even when the day had been fine and sunny, in spite of which I usually slept for about twelve hours. It may cause surprise that I was able to rest for so long in such circumstances, but it was largely a question of confidence. I was satisfied that the dinghy would stay above the waves which assailed it from all sides. I realized that if a wave should break inboard, the situation would be desperate but that the dinghy was unlikely to capsize. My reasoning was based on the comforting if somewhat over-simplified argument that if nothing happened during the day, I had nothing to fear during the night.

I had nothing to protect my head, as I only pulled up the tent as far as my neck, like a blanket, leaving my face open to a starlit sky such as I have never seen before or since. The light of the moon did duty as a friendly night-watchman's lamp.

The trade wind continued steady. I did not dare read too much for fear of having no way to occupy my time once I had run through my stock of books, which was already getting low. Although I continued to ship a little water from time to time, my things started to dry out. I took advantage of the better conditions to start my sums again, and every day seemed to tell the same optimistic story: you will land about the 23rd; you will land about the 23rd; you will land about the 23rd. I estimated my longitude at about 27° 30'. There seemed to be far fewer birds and not quite as many fish. It was now taking me two or two and a half hours a day to catch the necessary amount. There was still no sign of any floating seaweed, but then I was aiming to pass well to the south of the Sargasso Sea. It was clear that I was still drifting to the south because the signals from Dakar radio station gradually increased in strength. I was also making headway to the west, as I was starting to pick up some of the American stations. But the air waves over the Atlantic were monopolized by two nations: Britain and Russia.

Sunday, 2nd November, will remain in my memory because I did a very stupid thing. For some days my health had not been too good. The change of food and the constant humidity had caused a general skin eruption of painful little spots. I hoped to prevent them forming scabs by resting my weight on a little pneumatic cushion, the only one I had. Some clumsy movement must have knocked it overboard, a fact I only realized when I saw it floating a couple of hundred yards or so astern. I lowered the sail, put out the sea anchor and dived in to fetch it. I am a strong swimmer and reached the cushion in a few minutes. Imagine my horror, when I turned round, to see the dinghy sailing off without me, too fast for me to be able to catch it. The sea anchor, normally shaped like a parachute, had fouled itself and was no longer arresting the drift. It was quite clear that I would become exhausted long before I could overhaul it. At that moment L'Hérétique very nearly continued the voyage without me.

When I was training to swim the English Channel in 1951, in top physical condition, I once swam for twenty-one hours. Weakened as I was by privation and lack of exercise, I could not possibly have equalled the feat. I abandoned the cushion to its fate and concentrated on the fastest crawl of my life. Even in my race at Las Palmas with the elder Boiteux I am sure I never attained the same speed. I managed to cut down the distance a little, but then had difficulty in even maintaining it. Suddenly I saw L'Hérétique slow down. I caught it up and just managed to hoist myself on board. By a miracle, the cords of the sea anchor had disentangled themselves in the nick of time. I was physically and morally exhausted and swore it was the last dip I would take on the journey.

Relations with my marine neighbours assumed a definite pattern. They became almost like family friends. There were five or six dolphins and a petrel, which paid me a flying visit every day at four o'clock. It was a little black bird, its tail feathers tipped with white, about as large as a Paris sparrow. It baffled me how it had managed to cover such distances to seek its sustenance in the middle of the ocean. It approached from astern every day, sometimes settling down in the sea after four little steps on the water, and disappeared the moment the sun set. The dolphins were much more faithful and stayed

with me twenty-four hours a day. They were quite easy
to recognize. In trying to catch them with my bent knife
the first day, I had wounded them, and the marks still
showed. I noted with interest that fish, like human
beings, seem to heal slowly in sea-water. One of my
dolphins had an open place about the size of a half-crown
towards the end of its back, and another had been hurt
on one of its fins. There were five or six I recognized in
the same manner, and I gave them all names. The largest
one I called 'Dora'. She never left me, but took good care
not to come near enough for a second thrust. She cast a
fishy eye in my direction whenever she came near enough
to the boat, and sometimes turned on her side to look
at the sky. When the wind was slight and my speed
dropped, they used to take quick runs at the dinghy and
smack the floats with their tails, as if to ask why I was
lagging. They were joined regularly by newcomers, and
these were the ones I managed to catch. All I needed was
my bone hook, fixed to a length of string, baited with
the flying fish I picked up every morning on my tent. I
pulled the bait rapidly across the surface of the water, as
if it was a flying fish skidding over the surface before
diving again. The dolphins fairly fought for it, like dogs
for a bone, and one of them usually took the hook. All
the new arrivals fell for this trap, but my old friends,
knowing me too well, never as much as moved from
their tracks.

During the night of 3rd November, I caught in a flurry
of phosphorescence a long, thin, villainous-looking fish,
with a mouthful of vicious teeth which, by night,
seemed to drip a sort of whitish poison. Curiously
enough, in spite of the fight it had put up in the water,
after one final contortion, it seemed to go dead the
moment I pulled it aboard. Most fish flop around for
some time after they are landed. I assumed it was a fish

normally inhabiting great depths. Its eyes were huge in proportion to its head and its teeth enormous. I completely failed to identify it and in view of its menacing copper colour and the poisonous look of the slime it was dripping on my sleeping bag, where it had landed, I picked it up by the tail with immense care and threw it back in the water.

I learned later that it was a gempylus, the same sort of snake mackerel which landed on the sleeping bag of one of the members of the crew of the Kon-Tiki. The beast must have a particular affinity for sleeping bags. I used mine with a certain amount of care from then on, thinking with some trepidation of the organic poisons used by South American Indians to treat their arrows.

At eleven o'clock the next morning, a ship passed about a dozen miles away without seeing me. 'Pity the poor castaway,' I noted. 'He can count on no one but himself. I was between the ship and the sun and was not sighted, even though the vessel stopped a good ten minutes to take its position. I wish it had sighted me, as I could have got a reassuring message to my family. Its course was to the north-east, presumably on the route from America to the Azores.' (It must be remembered that I thought myself much further west than I was, and the ship was probably on its way from the Cape Verde Islands to the Canaries.)

If only I had known what the future held for me! A new error had started to creep into the calculations of my position. The Pilot Book gave me the hour of sunset for my latitude on the meridian of Greenwich. In theory, I should have added four minutes for every degree of longitude, and the same was nominally true for the times of the moon's rise and set. Now, although my estimated longitude did not correspond at all with the longitude given by the sun at midday and when it set, it did coincide exactly with that given by the time of the setting of the moon. I was quite incapable of explaining this discrepancy, and only learned the secret later from a French naval officer. It seems there is a problem of refraction involved.

I started to pass the time with little private parlour games, particularly with memory tests. Although I had never been a lover of arithmetic, I started to do immensely complicated sums in my head, dividing the two thousand seven hundred miles of my voyage by the number of miles I estimated for the day's run, in order to calculate how many days were left, and this I did half a dozen times or more, each time with a different divisor.

To add to the turmoil in my head, I became very superstitious about small things, the inevitable accompaniment of solitude. If I could not find my pipe the moment I looked for it, I considered it a bad omen. The little doll mascot, which my friends had given me on leaving the Canaries, began to acquire a tangible personality. I used to look at her and start a conversation, first of all in monosyllables, then whole sentences, describing exactly the next thing I was going to do. I did not wait for a reply, it was not yet a dialogue, although that would come; for the time being I just needed to assert myself. My dwindling stock of damp cigarettes created another superstition. Now and again I would try and light one. The number of matches I had to strike came to represent the number of days I would need to complete the voyage. Taking as point of departure the fact that I could not possibly arrive before 23rd November, I used to count as follows: if the first match caught light, I would arrive on the 23rd, the second meant arriving between the 23rd and the 25th, and so on. You can see how far a box could lead. If it took too long,

I used to discount the evidence: I was still an optimist
– that is to say, I accepted all the good auguries and
ignored all the bad ones. This is no bad basis for
contentment.

I began to know the exact sound of everything on
board at normal speeds, and when the wind was
moderate I used to estimate my speed by the exact note
of the sail's song. Although the wind had dropped for a
couple of days, it freshened again, and I appeared to be
making about four knots. If only I could keep it up I
would be there in twenty days. . . .

'Tuesday, 4th November. The moon sight gave me nine
degrees of difference from that of the sun and three
degrees from my estimated position. I am completely
baffled. My radio is working less well, and I can only
hear it during the evening hours, when conditions are
most favourable. I still take my estimated position as a
basis, with that given by the moon as an optimistic
possibility. Still steering due west and calculate I am on
latitude 18° 58′ north. Five months ago we were in
sight of Minorca, where we were to land the next day
at the end of our first lap. It seems a long time ago. By
1800 hours had caught no fish; particularly exasperating
as I am surrounded by pilot fish. By 1900 hours had
caught my dinner; at least I shall not have to fast during
the night. Visited by a magnificent white seagull and
surrounded by porpoises. Weather perfect, with the wind
driving L'Hérétique along at maximum speed with no
waves breaking inboard. If only this lasts.'

My urine was still perfectly normal and my general
health seemed good unless I compared it with my last
week on land. There would be many days, however, on
which the comparison would be even more marked.

The voyage was turning out more difficult and certainly more tedious than I had expected. However, at

the end of twelve days I expected to change the chart and start using that for the Caribbean approaches. That would mean I had eight hundred miles to go. The voyage from Casablanca to Las Palmas began to seem like child's play. I had finally given up any idea of showing a light at night. I may have missed thereby an occasion of sending news by a passing ship, and I began to brood about this during hours when I might have been reading. Somehow I had lost my taste for books and I felt I should have paid more attention, before leaving, to the old problem of what books to take on a desert island. (In order to have a little of everything, I had brought with me some Molière and a complete Rabelais, a Cervantes, a Nietzsche, Aeschylus in the two languages, Spinoza, a selection from Montaigne and, as musical scores, the two Passions of Bach and the Quartets of Beethoven.)

'I have no fear of a collision, the sea is absolutely empty. I will start showing a light at about 50° west, that is to say in about twelve days [sic], unless there is an increase in traffic before then.'

 ∞   ∞   ∞   ∞   ∞   ∞   ∞   ∞   ∞

On Wednesday, 5th November, I invented a new super- stition, meditating profoundly on the significance of Wednesdays in my voyage.

'Eighteenth day. Wednesdays have acquired a curious importance (or at least so I believe). I am sure that I shall arrive on a Wednesday.

Wednesday, 11th June, first lap to Ciudadela.

Wednesday, 18th June, returned to Ciudadela after the capsize.

Wednesday, 9th July, landing on Ibiza beach.

Wednesday, 16th July, entered harbour of Ibiza.

Wednesday, 23rd July, entered Motril harbour.

Wednesday, 13th August, left Tangier alone.

Wednesday, 20th August, arrived at Casablanca.

Wednesday, 3rd September, arrived in the Canaries.

Wednesday, 10th September, news of Nathalie's birth.

Wednesday, 24th September, arrived at Casablanca from Paris.

Wednesday, 1st October, presented with my radio.

And Wednesday, 5th November, half-way between Casablanca and the West Indies.'

I was being visited more frequently by sharks, but I had become quite used to them and treated them with complete disdain. They seemed a cowardly lot. A smart rap on the snout and they were off in a flash. They often came to prod the floats with their noses, and when I picked up an oar and clouted them on the head they never waited for more but plunged out of sight immediately. My dolphins must have been pleased, because they usually did a prudent disappearing act whenever there were sharks around. I must have gone up in their estimation because their numbers round L'Hérétique continually increased. But if they remained completely faithful, the pilot fish abandoned me when I met my first boat, the *Arakaka*. Always opportunists, they preferred the company of the strong.

That Wednesday, 5th November, I witnessed a remarkable spectacle. I had already seen a number of shoals of flying fish and most of the time they did just one glide over the surface of the sea; but when they were being attacked by the dolphins, they often took off again from the crest of a wave. Using their tails to pick up speed, they literally beat their fins to become airborne again in order to get away from their pursuers. The dolphins usually outwitted them. Skimming along with their dorsal fins breaking the surface, they managed to be on the spot where the flying fish touched the water again and the wretched creatures usually found a large open mouth waiting for them instead of a clear patch of sea.

That day the scene was even more extraordinary. Great shoals of flying fish were being attacked by a flock of shearwaters. I was mystified as to how there could be eleven shearwaters circling round me at such a distance from the coast. What I did not know was that at that moment I was almost within sight of the Cape Verde Islands.

All would have been well if my buttocks had not started to feel sore. I was afraid I might be developing boils. I also had a slight attack of parotitis, the inflammation of the salivary glands, of which the more severe and infectious form is mumps. However, I was still full of hope, and after four days I was able to note: 'Should arrive next week. Things could be worse, but I am starting to become obsessed with the idea of food. Promise myself an absolute feast of fruit when I arrive. Am getting tired of fish and birds.'

The castaway is always told that if birds appear in large numbers, land must be near. In this case it happened to be true, as land was only about sixty miles away (although it would have been quite impossible for me to head for it, in view of the prevailing wind and current). Another proverb of the sea is that land lies in the direction towards which the birds fly. The trouble was that when they left me, they flew off, not to the south-east, where the Cape Verde Islands lay, but to the west, where there was, in fact, no land for one thousand five hundred miles. It seemed an unkind way of nourishing my hopes.

My next entry read: 'Very hot; oh, for a good pint of

beer! My worst privation is undoubtedly the lack of real fresh water. I am sick of eating raw fish, but even more tired of drinking its juice. If only it would rain for a change. There are plenty of clouds in the sky and the sea is often rough, but there is no sign of rain. I have yet to see a drop.'

As a matter of fact, I was not thirsty; I just wanted a decent drink for a change, rather like a man who loses his appetite for macaroni but happily wolfs chicken. I had a nagging desire for fresh water, but it was not a question of physical suffering.

During the night of Thursday, 6th November, I was again attacked by a shark. He seemed to be a particularly tough customer and I could not keep him off – he must have acquired a taste for human flesh. I fixed my knife to the end of an oar while he butted away at the floats. I got ready to defend myself and the next time he turned on his back to attack at an angle I stuck the knife in him and slit him from throat to tail. The sea turned a blackish colour round him and I saw his entrails spilling out. My dolphins pounced on them. They always seemed hungry. For once, anyway, the hunter had become the hunted.

The fish must have found the dinghy an original and useful companion, as I was now surrounded by a veritable aquarium. I had never seen so many fish in all my life, even in the aquarium at Monaco. I hope there are some red faces among those who predicted that I would never catch a thing. Unfortunately my diet was giving me a mild form of diarrhoea. It certainly did not come from drinking sea-water, as it was some time since I had found this necessary.

I was writing up my log, when another shark appeared,

an absolute monster. It must have been nearly fifteen feet long. I grabbed my camera and started to turn the handle. It was a formidable-looking beast, looking absolutely ferocious, with a blunt snout and a huge mouth. I closed the valves between my floats as an emergency precaution. If it had managed to bite a chunk out of one of them, I would have to rely on the remaining four. But these beasts, cowards by nature, are much less aggressive during the day than at night. This one came to inspect my rudder oar and swam round me a few times, but otherwise kept his distance. I gave myself a figurative slap for my stupidity in diving after my pneumatic cushion a few days earlier. If a beast like this had attacked me, it would have been the end of the story.

I could still hear the radio at night, but it had become little more than a whisper, and half the time I had to put my ear to the loudspeaker. I could no longer make any check on the time in order to plot my position, and I had not learned to make use of the Pole Star. In any case, the sea-water had started to attack the mirrors in my sextant, and the Pole Star was not bright enough to show in it. I was now completely out of touch with the land, was deprived of news, and even started to forget what a human voice sounded like. The only voice and tangible presence left was my own, and my life started to resemble more and more that of the animals round me. I began to share their sensations and reactions, eating the same food and catching the same flying fish. My little petrel still kept up his four o'clock rendezvous, while the dolphins had become my protégés. We all tried to hide from the same sun, they in the shadow cast by the dinghy and I behind the sail during the afternoon. Like the fish, my point of reference became the wave, instead of the familiar path or row of trees by which the landsman finds his way.

It became almost impossible to realize that there were people on land living a regular life and attaching importance to such things as the clothes they wore. Under the broiling sun, the day more or less passed me by, I had returned to the primitive life. But I still felt a tingle in my spine on reading through my log, especially at the point where I was clearly starting to lose strength. I could see the change in my handwriting. The solitude was becoming increasingly oppressive and the log was my substitute for a human companion. Where I had filled a page or a page and a half each day at the beginning of the journey, I now scribbled two or even three and a half. I wrote little but often, and I was worried that I might run out of paper. Needing to sacrifice a book for purposes of my natural functions, I finally decided that the most apt was probably the Rabelais.

ᴑ   ᴑ   ᴑ   ᴑ   ᴑ   ᴑ   ᴑ   ᴑ   ᴑ

'Friday, 7th November. Twentieth day. The matches from the Canaries now refuse to light. Fortunately I still have a few boxes made in Morocco, and these still seem to work, even when soaked in sea-water and dried in the sun. But I shall have to go carefully with them.

'Calm night, regular wind, I slept well. Staying awake to check the time of moonrise, I was overcome by the feeling of what a strange and formidable element the sea is. It seems to form part of a system so entirely different from normal existence that it might belong to another planet. But there it is at my feet, alive yet inscrutable.

'Here and there lights appear in the depths, signs of a life only to be guessed at, but which seems intense. They look like stars half hidden in a cloudy night sky. The fish around me leap and swim to and fro, protagonists of an unseen and mysterious existence. Life at the surface is only the thin upper layer of another world.

'Twenty-first day. A little bubble of water appeared on one of the floats this morning, revealing a tiny air leak. I had a box of rubber patches, but the glue did not seem to hold. I used as substitute a substance of a more physiological nature. I hope I can spare the details by referring to the use to which I am putting my Rabelais. As long as it holds I am all right.'

Early morning and evening brought me a splendid catch of fish. I wondered how the experts would feel. How does one become an expert without any practical experience of a problem? Doubtless by extrapolation, but it is not a reliable scientific method.

The clouds were thickening, and I undressed in their pleasant shade. I examined my various small rashes, caused I assumed by perspiration, but my extremities were in good order and my physiological functions perfectly normal. I had grown the most tremendous beard. 'Ginette, my dear, I hope all this will be over soon. But still no ship in sight.'

That day I read the article on swordfish in my small encyclopaedia of fishing: 'The redoubtable adversary and scourge of the cetaceans; normally uses its sword to slash and not to spear as might be supposed, but when in a blind rage, as is sometimes the case, will attack ships with the point.' Hardly reassuring! I could only hope there was little likelihood of meeting one.

I began to think my compass was playing me up. My nominal course was 290°/280°, but the true course seemed to be about 260°, unless I was making much greater headway than I thought, and that I preferred to doubt. I expected soon to be on latitude 17° north. (I was on the parallel 17° 30') and intended to try and remain on it. I was particularly anxious to avoid the Doldrums, especially when only a hundred miles or so from the coast. The sea continued to show inexplicable moods. Usually the swell was slow and regular, but for no apparent reason and with no increase in the force of the wind, it would suddenly become choppy and irregular, and I had to watch the boat carefully. My dolphins were still with me and I was catching plenty of fish.

Time was beginning to weigh heavily, and I counted blindly and unhesitatingly on arriving during the week of the 23rd to 30th November. It never entered my head that December would still find me at sea.

On Saturday, 8th November, I noted at dawn 'large flock of birds', in spite of being, as I thought, a thousand miles from the nearest land. A number of flying fish, each about the size of a large sardine, landed in the dinghy, and would, I am sure, have tasted delicious fried. Even raw they were not so bad, and could have been taken for anchovies. My tame dolphins remained absolutely faithful, above all 'Dora', who seemed larger than ever and never gave me the slightest opportunity of catching her.

That day the sun was very strong, but the nights were cool and extremely pleasant. I could still just hear the radio, providing I did not have it on for more than ten minutes at a time, sufficient on that day to learn that there had been a storm over Boulogne and Dunkirk. Poor Ginette, I thought, how worried she must be. I wanted the whole thing to end as quickly as possible, more for her sake than for mine. My chief preoccupation was to lose no more latitude.

Then the radio went silent for good. I was on latitude 17° 14', which runs to the north of Guadeloupe between Antigua and Barbuda. I noted:

'Am always in a hurry for night to fall, first of all because it means another day gone, secondly because I can go to sleep trusting in Providence, and finally because I see nothing to upset me.'

This sort of passivity is typical of anyone who has been alone for a long time. He finishes by no longer dominating his surroundings, but bowing his head to whatever happens next. Any day not marked by some disturbing event is a good day, and an uneventful night is infinitely reassuring.

That day I was followed in the water by a long, green sausage, about ten feet long and nine inches or so in diameter. It was not a seaweed because it moved and wriggled. It finally cured me of any ideas of a swim.

The next day, 9th November, the fresh wind became even stronger. I was well pleased, as it pushed my speed up considerably, but I was worried about my patched sail. I got very wet during the night, and was afraid I would pay dearly for my swifter progress by helpless immobility if my sail carried away.

That was my fourth Sunday at sea, including the one on which I left. I hoped there would be only two more. From Monday, I was going to be able to talk to myself about 'next week'.

I had got tired of eating flying fish. In any case, they made a splendid bait for the dolphins and I could well do without them. During the night of the 9th and 10th, and during most of the following day, the wind remained strong. I was going along at a fine clip, but was haunted by the strain on the sail. For a whole week I had not seen another ship, but for the first time I caught a really big flying fish, about the size of a large mackerel. It was delicious.

'There are some big clouds gathering. It is going to be difficult to take my position tomorrow.'

Suddenly I was threatened again by the ever present danger of swamping. A wave broke near me and half filled the boat, momentarily threatening a capsize. By now I was convinced that if the worst happened, it would mean death. With this in mind, I had already put a little packet of barbiturates in my shirt pocket. I had made up my mind that if I was flung into the water, I was not going to fight it out for thirty hours or more. There was not the slightest possibility of receiving any sort of help. I thought the best thing was to put myself to sleep straight away.

Although it might be supposed that my senses had become deadened, my fears increased. I had been at sea for twenty days, always with the realization that one wave might finish me. The fact that the boat had at no time been in mortal danger made no difference. I was to remain at the mercy of that single wave until the last day of the voyage. I still thought it would only be another ten days before I reached the shipping routes, but until then there was no hope of succour.

CHAPTER XII

MID-PASSAGE

'LAND! LAND!' is the cry of the castaway when he sights the first coast. My cry on 11th November was 'Rain! Rain!'

I had noticed for some time that the surface of the sea had become strangely calm, exactly as if it were sleeked down with oil, and suddenly I realized why: 'Rain! Here comes the rain,' I cried aloud.

I stripped ready for it, so that I could wash all the salt off my body, and then sat down on one of the floats. I stretched out the tent on my knees, and held between my legs an inflatable rubber mattress, capable of holding some fifteen gallons of water. I waited. Like the sound of a soda syphon, monstrously magnified, I heard advancing from far away the noise of water beating on water. I must have waited nearly twenty minutes, watching the slow approach of this manna from heaven. The waves were flattened under the weight of the rain and the wind buffeted me as the squall hit the boat. The cloud passed over slowly, writhing with the vertical turbulence of a small cyclone. I was drenched in a tropical downpour, which rapidly filled the tent sheet and made it sag with the weight between my knees. I plunged my head in it and as quickly spat the water out again. It was impregnated with salt from the tent and I let it all spill overboard. At the second fill, although the water tasted strongly of rubber, it was like nectar. I washed myself voluptuously. The squall did not last long, but the rain-fall was tremendous. Not only did I drink my fill that day, but I was able to store three or four gallons in my rubber mattress. I was going to have a gurgling pillow, but each night my reserve of water was going to renew my hopes for the next day. Even if I had nothing to eat, even if I caught no fish, I at least had something to drink.

For three weeks I had not had a drop of fresh water, only the liquid I pressed from my fish, but my reactions were perfectly normal, just the marvellous sensation of swallowing a real drink at last. My skin was still in good order, although much affected by the salt, my mucous membranes had not dried, and my urine had remained normal in quantity, smell and colour. I had proved con-clusively that a castaway could live for three weeks (and even longer, because I could have continued perfectly well) without fresh water. It is true that Providence was to spare me the ordeal of having to rely again on the flat, insipid fish juice. From that day on I always had enough rainwater to slake my thirst. It sometimes seemed as if my stock was about to run out, but a shower always came in time.

I found that it was impossible to wash the salt out of my clothes and bedding, and I had to remain until the end 'a man of salt water' (as the Polynesians say of people who live off the sea) completely encrusted with it until the day of my arrival.

The day of the rain brought me both pleasure and per-turbation. The pleasure consisted in a new sort of bird, an attractive creature called, in English, I believe, a white-tailed tropic bird, and which the French call a *paille-cul*. It looks like a white dove with a black beak and has a long quill in its tail, which, with an impertinent air, it uses as an elevator. I rummaged quickly for my raft book, written for the use of castaways, and read that the appearance of this bird did not necessarily mean that one was near land. But as it could only come from the American continent, being completely unknown in the Old World, it was a good sign. For the first time, I had met a bird which came, without a shadow of doubt, from my destination.

This pleasant interlude was succeeded at about two o'clock in the afternoon by twelve hours of terror, which lasted until two the next morning. Just as I was peacefully reading a little Aeschylus, there was a violent blow on the rudder: 'That's another shark,' I thought, and looked up. What I saw was a large swordfish of undeniably menacing aspect. He was following the dinghy at a distance of about twenty feet, seemingly in a rage, his dorsal fin raised like hackles. In one of his feints round the boat he had collided with my rudder oar. I found I had a determined enemy. If I only succeeded in wounding him, he would surely attack again, and that would be the end of L'Hérétique. What was worse, as I was hurriedly getting my harpoon ready, a clumsy movement knocked it into the sea. It was my last one. Now I was disarmed. I fixed my pocket knife on to my under-water gun as a makeshift bayonet, determined to sell my life dearly if he attacked in earnest.

This intolerable anxiety lasted twelve long hours. As night fell I could follow the swordfish's movements by his luminous wake and the noise his dorsal fin made cutting the water. Several times his back bumped the underside of the dinghy, but he still seemed a little afraid of me. He never approached from ahead, and every time he came at me he changed course at the last moment before striking the floats. I came to believe that he was frightened, probably as frightened as I was. Every living creature possesses some means of defence, but it must perturb an attacker not to know what it is.

In the early hours of the morning his wake disappeared, but I spent a sleepless night.

One of the lulls in this encounter brought a minor relief, which I interpreted as a message from the land. It was one of those little glass floats used on fishing nets, encrusted with little shell-fish, cirripedia and other sorts of barnacle. It had clearly been in the water a long time, but it was a sign of human life.

It was an exhausting day, and by the time it was over I was utterly miserable. It rained so hard during the night that I thought I was going to have too much fresh water, after having gone without it for so long. I wrote: 'It would really be too much if I drowned in fresh water, but that is what is going to happen if this downpour goes on. I have enough for a month. My God, what a cloudburst! What is more, the sea is rising. A pale sun poked through this morning, but it is still raining.'

Another excitement was what I took to be my first clump of Sargasso seaweed. In fact, it was a magnificent jellyfish, the float blue and violet, of the type known as a Portuguese man-of-war. Its long treacherous filaments, hanging to a considerable depth, can cause dangerous stings, which often develop into ulcers.

I realized after one or two wakeful nights, how essential it was to get a good sleep: 'Forty-eight hours without sleep, and I am utterly depressed; the ordeal is really beginning to get me down. Moreover, the sea is infested with tunny and swordfish. I can see them leaping all round me. I do not mind the tunny and the birds so much, but the swordfish are a real menace. Am making good speed, but would willingly add another five or six days to the voyage if I could rest up in comparative calm. This dark, forbidding sea has a depressing effect.' It really seemed as if the sea was in mourning. It was as black as ink, flecked from time to time by a white crest, which the plankton made luminous by night. It looked like an evening dress with occasional white flowers, or a Japanese mourning robe. Not a star to be seen and the low sky seemed about to crush me. I realized the full meaning of the term 'heavy weather'; it felt like a physical weight on my shoulders.

At five o'clock on 12th November I noted: 'Rain and yet more rain, this is more than I can stand. But I wonder if I am not nearer the coast than I think, as there are several more birds. There are ten round me at the same time, and my bird book says that more than six mean that one is not more than a hundred or two hundred miles from the coast.' Little did I think that I was only just over a hundred miles away from the Cape Verde Islands.

∞   ∞   ∞   ∞   ∞   ∞   ∞   ∞   ∞

During the night of 12th and 13th November, I had another visit from a shark, or at least so I hoped. There was no way of telling whether it was a shark or a swordfish. Every time a shark appeared during the day, I felt perfectly safe. I gave it the ritual clout on the nose and off it went. But during the night, fearing that one of those devilish creatures might spear me with his sword, I was no longer able to be so bold. I had to remain watchfully awake, trying to identify the intruder, and waiting wide-eyed for it to make off. Sleep was effectively banished. And often it seemed that sharks or other creatures were playing some sort of ball-game during the night with my dinghy, without my daring to interfere.

It was still raining in torrents. Under such a deluge I was obliged to stretch the tent right over my head, but it formed great pockets of water which trickled down through the gaps. After a certain time the weight threatened to break the guy ropes, and I had to push from underneath to spill the water overboard. It must be difficult to realize the sacrifice involved for a castaway in thus jettisoning his reserve of fresh water. Even without sharks and swordfish, sleep had become practically impossible. The rain thundered down and every quarter of an hour or so I had to heave it overboard. An unbelievable quantity of water fell on the tent and trickled through every crevice.

I began to believe, in a confused sort of way, in the active hostility of certain inanimate objects. I might decide to write up the log or work out some calculation. I would sit down, with a pencil ready at hand. I only needed to turn round for ten seconds, and it found some means of disappearing. It was like a mild form of persecution mania, although up till then I had always been able to meet such annoyances with good humour, thinking of the similar misfortunes suffered by the Three Men in a Boat.

'Friday, 14th November. The last forty-eight hours have been the worst of the voyage. I am covered with little spots and my tongue is coated. I do not like the look of things at all. The storm has been short and violent. Was obliged to put out the sea anchor for several hours, but hoisted sail again at about 9.30. Raining in sheets and I am starting to get physically tired of the perpetual wetness, which there is no sun to dry. I do not think I have lost a great deal of time, but it is impossible to determine my latitude as I can see neither sun nor stars, and another of these confounded rain-storms is blowing up from the horizon. The sea is calmer, but yesterday I shipped plenty. They say, "fine weather follows rain". I can hardly wait for it.'

During the night a tremendous wave, catching me by the stern carried me along at great speed and then flooded

L'*Hérétique*, at the same time breaking my rudder oar. The dinghy immediately turned broadside on and my sail started to flap in a sinister manner, straining at my rough stitches. I plunged forward to gather it in, but stumbled against the tent and tore a great rent near the top of one of the poles. There would be no way of mending it properly and it happened just as I had to battle for life with the waves. I threw out both my sea anchors. Docilely, L'*Hérétique* turned her stern to my normal course and faced up to her assailants. By this time I was at the end of my strength and, accepting all the risks, I decided that sleep was the first necessity. I fastened up the tent as close as I could and made up my mind to sleep for twenty-four hours, whatever the weather did and whatever happened.

The squalls continued for another ten hours, during which my eggshell craft behaved admirably. But the danger was not yet passed. The worst moments came after the wind had dropped, while the sea continued to rage. The wind seemed to enforce a sort of discipline on the sea, propelling the waves without giving them time to break: left to themselves, they were much less disciplined. They broke with all their force in every direction, overwhelming everything in their path.

'*Saturday*, 15th *November*, 1330. Taking advantage of the rain to do a little writing. Have only two rudder oars left. Hope they will hold out. Rain has been coming down in torrents since ten o'clock yesterday evening, no sign of the sun; am wet through. Everything is soaked and I have no means of drying a thing, my sleeping bag looks like a wet sack. No hope of taking my position. The weather was so bad during the night that I wondered for a time if I had not drifted into the Doldrums. Fortunately there is no doubt that the trade wind is still with me. Making good time, almost too fast for comfort. Still worried

G

about the sail. When will the weather clear up? There was one patch of blue sky in the west, but the wind is from the east. Perhaps tomorrow will be better, but I am going to have another thick night. About seven o'clock this morning an aircraft flew over me quite low. Tried to signal it, but my torch would not work. First sign of human life since 3rd November, hope there will be more. Sky to the west now clearing rapidly, difficult to understand why.'

There was a sort of battle in the sky the whole day between the two fronts of good and bad weather. I called it the fight between the blue and the black. It started with the appearance in the west of a little patch of blue, no bigger than a gendarme's cap, as the French song has it, and there seemed little hope of it growing. The black clouds, impenetrable as ink, seemed fully conscious of their power, and marched in serried ranks to attack the tiny blue intruder, but the blue patch seemed to call up reinforcements on its wings, and in a few hours to the south and north, that is to say to my left and right, several more blue patches had appeared, all seemingly about to be engulfed in the great black flood advancing towards them. But where the clouds concentrated on frontal attacks, the blue of the sky used infiltration tactics, breaking up the mass of black until the good weather predominated. By four o'clock in the afternoon its victory was clear. 'Thank God for the sun! I am covered with little spots, but the sun is back.' Little did I know that the most troublesome part of my voyage was about to begin.

I had not the faintest idea where I was. With no sun for three days I was in a state of complete ignorance, and on Sunday the 16th when I got my sextant ready, I was in a fever of apprehension. By a miracle I had not drifted much to the south. I was still on latitude 16° 59′, which passes to the north of Guadeloupe. That vital point was settled, but my boat looked like a battle-field. My hat had blown off in the storm and all I now had as protection for my head was a little white floppy thing, made out of water-proofed linen, quite inadequate in such a climate. The tent was torn in two places and although the dinghy seemed to have suffered no damage, everything in it was drenched. Even after the long sunny days which were now to come, the night dew continued to re-impregnate my warm clothes and sleeping bag, so I was never again to know a dry night until I touched land.

A disturbing incident then showed that I could not afford to relax my vigilance for one moment. During the storm, I had tried to protect the after part of L'Hérétique from the breaking waves by trailing a large piece of rubberized cloth fixed firmly to the ends of my two floats. This seemed to divert the force of the waves as they broke behind me. Even though the storm had died down, I saw no point in removing this protection. But the following night, a frightful noise brought me out of my sleeping bag at one bound. My protective tail was no longer there. The piece of cloth had been torn away. I checked anxiously that the floats had not been damaged and that they were still firmly inflated. Some creature which I never saw, probably attracted by the vivid yellow of the cloth which hung down between the floats, and torn it off by jumping out of the water. This it had done with such precision that there was no other visible sign of its attack.

Like the boat, I too had taken a buffeting. I was much weakened and every movement made me terribly tired, rather like the period after my long fast in the Mediter-ranean. I was much thinner, but was more worried about the state of my skin. My whole body was covered with tiny red spots. At first they were little more than surface discolorations, not perceptible to the touch, but in a day or two they became hard lumps that finally developed into pustules. I was mortally afraid of a bad attack of boils, which, in the condition I was in, would have had serious consequences. The pain alone would have proved unbearable and I would no longer have been able to sit or lie down.

The only medicament I had to treat such an outbreak was mercurochrome, which made me look as if I was covered in blood. During the night the pain became very bad and I could not bear anything in contact with my skin. The least little abrasion seemed to turn septic and I had to disinfect them all very carefully. The skin under my nails was all inflamed, and small pockets of pus, very painful, formed under half of them. I had to lance them without an anaesthetic. I could probably have used some of the penicillin I had on board, but I wanted to keep up my medical observations with a minimum of treatment for as long as I could stand it. My feet were peeling in great strips and in three days I lost the nails from four toes.

I would never have been able to hold out if the deck had not been made of wood, which I regard as an essential piece of equipment in a life-raft. Without it I would have developed gangrene or, at the very least, serious arterial trouble.

For the time being my ailments were still localized. My blood pressure remained good and I was still perspiring normally. In spite of that, I greeted with relief the victorious sun which appeared on the 16th, expecting it to cure the effects of the constant humidity which I had endured. I did not know that the sun was to cause even worse ordeals during the cruel twenty-seven days which were to follow.

The castaway must never give way to despair, and

should always remember, when things seem at their worst, that 'something will turn up' and his situation may be changed. But neither should he let himself become too hopeful; it never does to forget that however unbearable an ordeal may seem, there may be another to come which will efface the memory of the first. If a toothache becomes intolerable, it might almost seem a relief to exchange it for an earache. With a really bad pain in the ear, the memory of the toothache becomes a distinctly lesser evil. The best advice that I can give is that whether things go well or ill, the castaway must try to maintain a measure of detachment. The days of rain had been bad enough, but what followed, in spite of the rosy future the sun at first seemed to promise, was to seem much worse.

The 16th November was my twenty-ninth day at sea, and I had every reason for optimism. There had been a decline in my health, but at least the worst part of the journey was now behind me. Up till then I had had to maintain a course across the wind, but now I was sailing directly before it. I had collected enough fresh water for about a month, and the fish which had accompanied me from the start still surrounded the boat. The old hands, those that I had succeeded in wounding during the first few days, had not forgotten their experience and remained out of reach. Every morning I saw them rise from the depths, give me a suspicious look, and then take up their position on a parallel course. Their company became increasingly welcome, partly because they were old friends, and even more because they encouraged other fish to join them. The newcomers arrived in shoals, duped by their more cunning relations, and sported all around me, providing an endless supply of innocent victims.

Certain 'specialists' had advised me to install a small

tank in the bottom of the boat in which to keep the fish
I caught. The reader will by now appreciate how super-
fluous was such advice. My larder followed me wherever
I went. Not only that, but my faithful dolphins chased
unlimited flying fish in my direction. They scared them
into flight so that they crashed into my sail, and I picked
up five or ten every morning. They never landed in the
dinghy during the day, presumably because they saw me
and could avoid the obstacle, but I could watch them all
the time, as there was never an interval of more than five
minutes before a squadron or two took the air. The
ingenuity and skill with which the dolphins chased them,
after flushing a covey, was a spectacle of which I never
got tired. With wide-open mouths they usually managed
to be at the exact spot where the flying fish hit the water
again. A few of the intended victims, probably taught
by experience, changed direction in mid-air, and by
bouncing from one wave crest to another managed to
elude their pursuers.

∽   ∽   ∽   ∽   ∽   ∽   ∽   ∽   ∽

Once the storm was over, I carried out an under-water
inspection of the dinghy, with a secure lifeline round my
waist. Almost all the repairs effected at Las Palmas had
succumbed to the battering of the sea. The glue had not
held, and strips of rubberized fabric fluttered down
lamentably. A whole colony of cirripedia, a type of
barnacle, had affixed themselves along the seams. Of all
the experts familiar with my type of boat, only M.
Debroutelle, the manufacturer of the dinghy, and a real
specialist in everything that concerned it, had warned
me: 'You cannot expect to avoid barnacles.'

The one detail of construction of L'Hérétique which I
considered a potential weakness was the seams which

connected the sections of fabric. There was little likelihood of the floats bursting from internal pressure. Every
seam had been covered with a safety band, but it was
still possible for these tiny shellfish to penetrate underneath it, tearing it loose as they grew. I had already
noticed at Tangier that even when the dinghy was moored
in a deep bay, a dense submarine growth attached itself
to the bottom, particularly along the seams. The main
seams held the sternboard in position between the rubber
bottom and the floats, and secured the floats to the rubber
bottom.

From Casablanca to the Canaries, the depth of the
water and the speed at which I travelled arrested the
growth of these marine parasites, but during the time I
spent at Las Palmas, the bottom of the dinghy became
covered with an absolute forest of seaweed and barnacles.
After I had scraped them off, I noticed with foreboding
the little bumps under my safety bands where some of
the organisms had penetrated. and I therefore stuck on a
double layer. These were precisely the points where the
fabric had given way from the effect of the storm. I could
carry out no further repairs under water, and had no
option but to trust in the confidence which M. Debroutelle had in his boat, and climbed back inboard without
much difficulty.

CHAPTER XIII

LONGITUDE

∽ ∽ ∽ ∽ ∽ ∽ ∽ ∽ ∽ ∽

'SUNDAY, 16TH NOVEMBER. It is now four weeks since I left, a whole month, and have been able to take my latitude for the first time in four days. In spite of everything, I have remained on the seventeenth parallel (16° 59′, to be exact). This is perfect: I shall land some-where between Guadeloupe, Montserrat and Antigua. With any luck, I should arrive between Saturday 22nd and Saturday 29th November, the two extreme limits of time, providing all goes well. Something bumped me again during the night; I do not know what it was, but the pieces of fabric I had fixed again to prevent waves breaking into the boat have been torn away. There must be some unpleasant company around. Hot sun, but plenty of spray.

'Four o'clock. Another swordfish, confound it! But this one is quite small. He made one quick turn round me and then made off, but I still do not like it.

'Monday, 17th November. Wind only light during the night, but sea very rough. This morning I understand why: a fine storm is blowing up. The whole eastern sky looks threatening. Plenty of birds.

'Four o'clock. Managed to take my approximate position all right, but it is by no means easy in such a heavy sea. Wind has picked up and I am making good speed. The next few days are not going to be easy and I am by no means confident that I have calculated my position correctly. If only I could meet a boat so that I could confirm it! Theoretically I only have about five hundred miles to go. It would be unbearable to fail now. Sometimes I want the week to end and at others I do not. Sky looks threatening, but good speed is the main thing. Should sight land in six days if all is well. Feel tired and would like above all: (1) a hot bath, (2) watertight shoes, (3) a dry bed, (4) a roast chicken, (5) a quart of beer.

'Still plenty of flying fish; not daring to put out lines in case I catch a swordfish and make him lose his temper. Am also putting off the moment for showing a light at night; the danger of a swordfish attack seems greater than that of being run down. Do not like look of the sea. Feel afraid of it, more so than at the start. Curiously, the sea is not at its most dangerous when the waves are high, only when it is not controlled by the wind. It is dangerous when a storm is gathering, because it is not yet under control, and also when the storm has blown itself out and no longer gives the sea a rhythm. I am going to pass a bad night, I can see that.

'*Tuesday*, 18th *November*. Morale higher today, but time is beginning to weigh. Have started to think about the problem of landing. If I keep on this latitude I shall end up either at Port-Louis or Pointe-à-Pitre in Guadeloupe. All the harbours are protected from the wind and difficult for me to enter, but if I miss Pointe-à-Pitre I shall be in the Caribbean Sea. If I am north of latitude 16° 30', I shall try for the north coast, either Desirade or Marie Galante. Cannot bear the idea of having some accident while landing and prefer not to think about it. Sufficient unto the day . . .! Decide to send off a message in a bottle; it will be amusing to see if it is picked up.

'*Wednesday*, 19th *November*. Had a shock when I took my latitude; found I had been carried twenty miles to the south, compared with yesterday. Found, after a check, that I had misread the sextant. Thank goodness for that.

* G

After the midday sight, the long afternoon hours. Am fishing again and catch all I need in the morning, so there is nothing left to do but ruminate on the possible day of my arrival. Getting very bored. Sun scorching, but weather uncertain. Continue to do my daily physical check-up and still have something to read. More rain this morning.

'Thursday, 20th November. Steering due west on latitude 16° 48', which should bring me between Guadeloupe and Antigua. If I can maintain this, will try and land on Guadeloupe, which is French territory. Spent one of the best nights of the voyage; plenty of birds. One thing makes me feel I must be getting near land: the wind blows from eight o'clock to eleven-thirty, when it drops, freshening again at three o'clock. This, I remember, is the pattern near the coast. Must concentrate entirely on keeping this course. Probably have another week to go, but at least until then promise myself not to despair. Poor Ginette must be worried to death. For her sake I would like to get there as soon as possible.

'Friday, 21st November. The nearer I think I am, the more doubts I have about my exact position, but it ought to be correct. Still no sign of a ship, but I must remember that on the way to the Canaries I saw only two, and those quite close to land. Take heart from the birds, which I see flying off to the east in the morning and flying back towards the west in the evening, presumably on their day's flight from the land. This seems a good sign. Weather variable, but quite good, wind uneven. Am in a real hurry to get there. Have decided to show a light at night, and it brings me an absolute shower of flying fish. Must arrive between Saturday 22nd and Saturday 29th. Monday, Tuesday or Wednesday are the most likely days. Still on latitude 16° 48'. Good!

'Saturday 22nd November. Very little wind, I am crawling

like a tortoise. At this speed it will take at least another week. As I feared, these days are proving a great strain. In spite of myself, I do nothing but scan the horizon. Every cloud looks like the first shadow of land, although I know I cannot possibly see any until Monday. So avid for the sight of it that I am prepared to remain on watch for a week. Large increase in the number of land birds, that must mean something. Still no sign of a ship. Wind has picked up, praise God.

'1300 hours. Heat tropical; how poor Ginette must be suffering, morally and physically. "My dear, in another four or five days your worries will be over." If only the trade wind would freshen!

'1730 hours. If the wind remains like this it will take me ten days to sight land.

'Sunday, 23rd November. Sixth Sunday at sea, can only hope it is the last. The wind has picked up and seems steady; if it keeps that way I shall arrive Tuesday or Wednesday, but cannot tell where, as I am drifting somewhat to the northward. Have sighted a couple of curious creatures that look like trigger fish, but their two fins resemble those of a shark. Tried to catch one of them, but without success. Pity; am getting a little tired of flying fish.

'1700 hours. A small storm is brewing to the south-west. No half measures about this weather; either a burning sun without a cloud in sight or a thunderstorm. The wretched fish, nibbling at my barnacles, keep butting the bottom of the boat, a most disagreeable feeling. The storm is now gathering, I hope it does not hit me too hard. Not too worried, however fierce it is, as I cannot be far from my destination now. Saw three white-tailed tropic birds together this morning, and my castaway's handbook says that this means that land cannot be more than eighty miles away. Just as the storm reached me, a frigate bird flew over. Another encouraging note in the handbook: "The frigate bird never spends the night at sea and is seldom found more than a hundred miles from land. In one exceptional instance, one was sighted three hundred miles from the nearest coast." At two o'clock in the afternoon I saw a northern gannet not very far away, another bird seldom seen more than ninety miles out to sea. All this confirms that I cannot have far to go.'

Before the storm clouds started to gather on the horizon I had begun to feel curiously uneasy. Perhaps that is not the right word, but I felt a strong compulsion to flee, to get away from where I was. I could not tell why, but I would have liked to have found myself somewhere else, and quickly at that. There was little to distinguish my situation from that of the creatures in the sea round me, and I must have acquired some part of their instincts. I took out my Pilot Book to read the section dealing with indications of a typhoon. I scrutinized every point of the compass and saw only gold flecks in the sky and a few black patches gathering on the horizon, nothing alarming, but I still felt that something unpleasant was going to happen. I felt quite unable to escape what I was sure was some impending catastrophe making straight for me. Some time after I arrived in Barbados I discovered that in a number of ships a hundred miles or so to the north, the crews had experienced the same feeling of disquiet. There is a subtle but powerful communion of thought processes amongst those who ply the sea.

Right across the horizon behind me, only just visible, appeared a line of black, as if drawn with a ruler, seeming to prevent the sun from rising. There was a slow drop in the temperature, and the black line advanced across the sky like an awning. Starting at six o'clock in the morning, it did not complete its slow progress until seven o'clock in the evening, but it did not seem to be preceded by any freshening of the wind. The sea remained calm and I thought I would be able to keep my sail hoisted and weather the approaching storm. Then I heard a characteristic noise I knew well, like a forest fire or a machine-gun; rain was pouring down from the black mass, sounding like thousands of fir-cones thrown into a fire. Very soon the gale was upon me, with a sudden buffet of wind which somehow did not seem part of it but was no less violent for that. I made up my mind to take advantage of it for as long as possible, holding the main sheet of my sail in my hand, ready to let it go if the pressure proved too great. Day was turned into night, and while the raindrops flashed on the surface of the sea, my sail suddenly filled like a balloon. The storm did not rage for long, but was terrifying while it lasted. For an hour, with the main sheet wrapped round my wrist, I tore through the fury of the elements at five knots or more, and when it was over my hand was covered in blood from the friction of the rope. With no transition period, the moment the rear edge of the storm-cloud passed over me, the wind disappeared completely, and for the first time since I had left the Canaries the sail started to flap, and then dropped, inert. I was convinced that the worst was now over and the long period of bad weather, strong winds and excessive spray at an end. I was to experience yet another evil that beset the days of sail, a prolonged dead calm. I think the notes I made in my log-book at the time express better than any subsequent commentary the anguish into which this exasperating state of affairs was to plunge me.

'Monday, 24th November. I was right: one should not count one's chickens before they are hatched. After the storm, there is only a faint breeze coming from due south. With the drift, I am having serious trouble in maintaining a compass route even of 320°, and I am being carried dangerously to the north. I am terribly afraid of getting caught in the Gulf Stream and carried northwards. (It must not be forgotten that I still thought I had arrived roughly at the junction of the northern Equatorial Current and the Gulf Stream.) This would mean another month. Feeling very disheartened. If I get carried up to latitude 23° or 24° I shall be frozen, as winter is now upon us. If only I could meet a ship! The wind must change. And to think that I only had ninety miles to go! This could only happen to me. The trade wind seems to have completely disappeared. Am terribly afraid there will be days and days of this, and I was so near.

'1500 hours. Weather conditions still the same, but am feeling a little better. I see in the Pilot Book that these disturbances are only temporary and the trade wind soon re-establishes itself. Nevertheless, have lost a lot of time. Guadeloupe is now at least a hundred miles away, and I may now have to make either for Barbuda, 17° 40' north, 61° 50' west, a hundred and twenty miles away; Barbados, 13° 10' north, 59° 30' west, or even Puerto Rico, four hundred miles away. That is to say, either another week, providing the wind returns, or anything up to six months. Am, in fact, nineteen minutes of latitude further north, on the parallel which passes between Barbuda and Antigua. If only the weather would change. What filthy luck, just as I was nearly there. If only I could sight a ship! But there is nothing, absolutely nothing in sight.

'Tuesday, 25th November. The wind has veered a little and is now blowing from the ESE. Have been able to regain about eleven miles to the south, and am now on latitude 17° 05', on a better course. That is not too bad, but fear the next few days may be very difficult and depressing after all this delay. If my calculations of longitude are right, I am only sixty miles from the nearest land, but cannot be sure. Must see land tomorrow, otherwise I shall have no idea where I am. My course is all right, but I shall have no idea how far I have progressed along it. Taking the most pessimistic estimate, I could be about seven degrees further east, about four hundred and six miles away, or six days' sailing at this speed. Must not lose heart before Tuesday, 2nd December. If nothing has happened by then, I shall be completely baffled. How long the days are! Even my four o'clock petrel has disappeared; he paid me a visit the day before yesterday, but I did not see him yesterday for the first time during the voyage. I wonder if he flew back to land or further out to sea. For all I see of them, every ship in the world might have sunk and every aircraft crashed.

'Wednesday, 26th November. Saw two more frigate birds this morning, so land should be less than a hundred miles away, if what is said about them is true. Perhaps I am right about my position after all. Visibility poor, as it was near the Canaries, only about fifteen miles, and these islands are thirty miles apart. Hope there will be no repetition of what nearly happened in the Canaries, when I almost passed between them without seeing either. If I know I have passed them, I will steer north-west for Puerto Rico. If there is no means of telling, then anything may happen. And to think that the day before yesterday visibility must have been at least forty miles. Damn that storm! Am still trying to get back to the latitude of Guadeloupe and stay between 16° and 16° 30′ north.

'1500 hours. Crawling like a tortoise. I cannot be more than sixty miles from Antigua and am hardly moving. If I am making thirty miles a day, it would be a miracle. These last two hundred miles could have been measured by the yard, but this cannot last more than forty-eight or seventy-two hours [!]. Now that I really seem near, time is passing more slowly than ever. Am incapable of realizing that it is possible, even probable, that by this time on Tuesday I shall be on *terra firma*. I just cannot picture it.

'*Thursday, 27th November.* This slowness is exasperating. I would be lucky to have made twenty miles since Sunday. It is beginning to look more like Tuesday or Wednesday week, another ten days of torture. I have really had enough, and with this visibility am in constant fear of missing the islands. It is a terrible strain to keep scanning the horizon. My eyes are focusing on it all the time and I have no dark glasses to reduce the glare of the sun. No ships, no planes, no birds. *I have had enough* [underlined in my log]. Forty days is enough for any man.

'1800 hours. Caught a fly in the boat; this must be a good sign. Land cannot be far away.

'*Friday, 28th November, 9 o'clock.* Still nothing in sight this morning, am really getting perturbed. Poor Ginette, forty-one days and no news of me. But my sight at moonset confirmed that land can only be sixty miles away. I am on the right latitude, but hardly making any headway. Passed a lamp bulb, of all curious things, floating in the water. Am absolutely browned off.

'1900 hours. Quite a nice fresh little breeze, better than anything for a week. If it keeps up, I should sight land within eighteen hours. No sign of a ship since Monday, 3rd November.

'*Saturday, 29th November.* That breeze lasted exactly ten minutes; sky leaden; temperature a hundred degrees under my tent, no wind, no land, no ship, no plane, no birds; desperate.

'Am hardly making way, probably half a mile an hour. This is going to take another ten or twenty days, although I was told that the trade wind blew right across. Alarmed at the thought of how anxious my family must be. If only I could meet a boat which would pass on news of me,

but there is absolutely nothing to be seen. Caught a
trigger fish today with my knife on the end of an oar;
hesitate to eat it as one book calls it edible and another
poisonous. Prefer to take no risk. You would think that
those who have studied the problems of castaways would
agree about something.

'1900 hours. Wind springs up just as it did yesterday.
If only it would last. Launched another message in a
bottle. Boat followed by a large barracuda, a new sort of
fish, so land must be near. Try to catch him, but he
avoids me with a dirty look. Think he would probably
like to eat me.

'Sunday, 30th November. A whole week of near immobility. Confound the wretches who said the trade wind
would blow all the way. Eight days of calm, nothing in
sight. Have a bad attack of diarrhoea which obliges me to
squat over the side twenty times a day. The trade wind is
a snare and a delusion, it takes you three-quarters of the
way across and then abandons you. And this is supposed
to be the best time of year for it. Must resign myself.
Supposing I had made thirty miles a day, that would give
me an average of fifty-five miles a day since the start.
This means arriving on Sunday, 7th December, another
week. Patience. But then I give up.

'Monday, 1st December. So there I am. November over and
still no sight of land. Prey to every emotion. The hour of
moonrise would seem to put me on 50° of longitude
and its setting on 60°, am absolutely foxed. Full moon
tonight, we shall see. Making some headway with a
light breeze which has sprung up, but it was flat calm
during the whole night. Am I forty or twelve hundred
miles away? Real torrid heat, horizon empty and hazy.
If only I knew my longitude for certain, had a battery for
the radio set and a proper chronometer. Had a morning
visit from a white-tail, which nearly alighted on a float.

Took a snap of him but when I got out my cine-camera he took fright and flew off into the sun.

'1100 hours. Knowing her as I do, am really worried about Ginette; she must be thin and miserable, and there may be another ten days of this. Worn out and anxious myself, this diarrhoea is starting to get me down. Signs of blood in the stool, hope it is nothing serious.

'1500 hours. Latitude still perfect; something of a breeze and a frigate bird, the fourth in five days, has arrived to cheer me up. As three hundred miles out is apparently their maximum, and I have been seeing them for five days, I cannot have much more than a hundred miles to go. Hope springs eternal.

'1800 hours. Have just looked through my pictures of France, Casablanca and Las Palmas. It was a mistake. Now I am really depressed. The ordeal has gone on too long and this uncertainty about my position is the last straw. I must be right within two hundred miles or so, but shall I arrive the day after tomorrow, or in ten, twenty or thirty days? I have no idea and am beginning to wish I had stopped in the Canaries. Then my pride reproaches me. If only I could sight a ship. If I could hear the radio I would be less alone. As for those who assured me that the wind would blow from the north-east right till the end, I'll get even with them yet. Since the storm, there has either been no wind at all, or it has come from the south-east.

'*Tuesday, 2nd December.* [My morale was very low and the log is quite difficult to decipher.] Still nothing in sight; saw a new type of bird this morning, a Manx shearwater, also described as not flying more than a hundred miles out to sea.

'This seems to be the evidence for and against the proximity of land:

'Against: hour of sunrise, sunset, zenith and moonrise.

But the first three already showed an error of about an hour on my departure, when I knew my longitude. The hour of moonrise would put me at about 50° west, but this is contradicted by the reading given when it sets.

'For: Hour of moonset, which makes me about 60° west, irregularity of the wind which falls at night, frigate bird, few birds in general, but new types and not a single albatross. I have made fifty or sixty miles a day, which was my average on the first lap to the Canaries, that is to say between 2,000 and 2,400 miles; there can only be between 180 and 380 miles to go.

'At best, I am at longitude 59° or 60°, at worst only at 50°.

'If the wind had held, I would have been ashore a week ago, but it is extremely light, and only blows five or six hours a day, less than between Tangier and Casablanca. It looks as if I shall never cover the remaining two or three hundred miles. Nothing is more exasperating than to have logged 2,500 in a month and then need thirty days for the remaining 300. Still no sign of a wind, it is really too much. Am beginning to lose hope completely. My experiment has now lasted forty-four days, but I cannot bear the idea of failure so near success. If only I could pass on some news, but have seen neither plane nor boat. As for the Raft Book, all its information about birds is tripe and serves only to lower one's morale.

'1500 hours. What I fail to understand is this: my chief problem should have been to avoid drifting too far south, but for ten days that is where what wind there is has come from. What has happened to the north-east trade wind? Now forty-five days out, a month and a half, and Ginette still completely without news. Another day lost. Fortunately few of them have been as cloudless as this, otherwise my skull would soon be at boiling point. Looks like another storm blowing up.

'Wednesday, 3rd December. Absolutely disgusted. The wind has swung round to the north-east again, after first veering west, a charming touch, but it is pretty feeble.

'1100 hours. Wind suddenly freshens for the first time in a week. If only it lasts.

'1500 hours. Stock of fresh water getting low. Need rain, but not too much!

'1800 hours. Another frigate bird; have given up counting how many I have seen. If the Raft Book is right, and they do not venture beyond a hundred miles, then I hope that this time it is correct. If it had been true about the others, I would already be there. Diarrhoea now very bad and seems to make me terribly thirsty. Would love to drink a quart of milk, just like that, at one gulp.

'Thursday, 4th December. Nothing in sight, not a thing. Am beginning to feel physically exhausted. Visited today by a butterfly. Also saw a gossamer thread floating in the air, such as spiders spin on land. Surely after that land cannot be far away. Score for ships and 'planes: nil.

'Friday, 5th December. For all I know the land is only a few dozen miles away, but that doesn't help me as I still have no wind. Am worn out with this continuing diarrhoea and haemorrhage. I hardly dare to eat any more; if this goes on, the boat may arrive, but they will find me in it dead. Sky still leaden, not a cloud to be seen. Am completely baffled, have no idea where I am. If the dinghy is thrown up with me as a corpse, I have only one request, and that is that someone goes and boxes the ears of the author of this Castaways' Handbook. It only serves to demoralize anyone who has been unfortunate enough to buy it. It states in black and white: "A considerable number of frigate birds means that land is about a hundred miles away." I have seen quite a number during the last week and have covered about three hundred miles. The only moral is that the author is dishonest to make statements he knows to be false, or if he has not confirmed them then he should leave them out. The same applies to those who make assertions about the trade wind. It is perfectly clear that they have never had to make the journey themselves, or else they were in a ship with an engine. In the area of the West Indies, in November and December, there are two days of wind for every ten days of flat calm.

'Problem for the day: assuming that I am making a hundred yards an hour, how long will it take me to cover the hundred miles to land, if such a place exists. I shall be dead first, either burnt to a crisp, or a victim of thirst and hunger. Everything seems to conspire against me. Since this morning I have literally been stewing in my own juice under a terrible sun. No shade, and yet barely half a mile away the sky is covered with thick clouds. It is frightening to realize to what extent one can develop a persecution mania alone on the surface of the sea; it really seems as if one is the victim of a conspiracy which one will never defeat. The wind is propelling several small cloud formations but it seems as if they deliberately avoid the sun rather than pass across it and give me a little shade.

'I am exhausted. If I fail it will be because everything has turned against me; no wind and a scorching sun. Yesterday it rained all round the horizon but not a drop fell into the boat, it really is too much. My sail is flapping from left to right, so much for the trade wind. Definition of the trade wind area: a region where there is practically never any wind. I cannot even explain it by saying that I am in the Doldrums. At this time of year they lie about latitude 5° north, and in that case I would already have sighted land. This diarrhoea is unbearable. One thing I know, the next time there is a storm, I will trust in God, and under no circumstances put out the sea anchor. What have I done to deserve all this? After all, I could perfectly well have stopped in the Canaries.

'Jean Luc, if I am dead on arrival, please publish a book made up of these entries as a small recompense to my wife. I was right when I said it was a bad omen when seamen said that this crossing was possible. Mediterranean, Casablanca, the Canaries, were easy, although they were described as impossible. And now I am going to fail lamentably. How pleased a lot of people are going to be. I cannot stand the noise of this flapping sail . . . this is the worst day of all; I would prefer a good storm. Have thrown some fluorescent stuff in the water, which makes a stain in the sea, in order to see how long I can keep it in sight. I may be making better time than I think. What really worries me is that up till now, even when I had very little wind, the clouds always indicated there was some at high altitudes. Today I do not even have that consolation. I hope this does not go on for another week. It is now thirty-two days since I saw a ship, and twenty-one since I sighted a plane; am utterly despondent. To think that Jack said, "We shall never make it because of the wind, storms and hurricanes"; but it is this flat calm which has caused disaster. If only I could send an SOS! But that is quite impossible. Not a single cloud passes across the sun, although there are plenty of them. I do not understand what is going on; now there are lots of little flecks of low cloud racing across the sky, but I am still in a dead calm such as I have seldom seen, not even in the Mediterranean. If only I could have a bath.

'Saturday, 6th December. Quite a fresh breeze from the north, it is better than nothing. I saw three more whitetails together this morning; I can only suppose that land is sixty or eighty miles away. I cannot believe that the author of the Castaways' Handbook is wrong every time; perhaps, after all, I shall see land tomorrow or the day after. Come what may, I would like to record my last wishes, in case I am dead when the boat arrives:

'1 I desire these notes to be made into a book, the rights to be held by Ginette Bombard, my wife. The following may be consulted on the background and reasons for this voyage: [then I listed several names].

'2 [Here I gave certain instructions concerning provision for my wife and daughter.]

'3 Steps must be taken to prevent the death of other castaways whose morale has been shattered by the authors of handbooks giving false information about signs of the proximity of land. Moreover, I hold responsible for my death those who prevented me from having the radio transmitter I so badly need at the moment.

'My thesis holds good for a duration of fifty days. If I am dead on arrival, there is no need for other castaways to despair. After that period, the strain on the human system is too great. It is highly desirable that astronomy courses in schools should include instruction in the principles of practical navigation.

'Sunday, 7th December. Still nothing in sight, but I cannot be far away now. [At this point my writing becomes stronger and more legible.] I must get there alive, if only for Ginette, Nathalie, Renaud and Anne, but this suspense is terrible.

'The sun is implacable, and I am very thirsty. My supply of fresh water is running low, there cannot be more than about a gallon left; and to think how much I have thrown overboard! Barrels and barrels of it! Am doing very little fishing, but catching enough. With this horrible diarrhoea, cannot bear the thought of having to start drinking sea-water and fish juice again, am really feeling quite ill. Yesterday's north wind drove me eighteen miles to the south, carrying me away from

Désirade, the nearest land; now it has dropped again, it is almost too much to bear. And there it stands in the Pilot Book (West Indies, Volume 2, lines 9–14): "the trade wind is at its strongest and most regular from December to March or April. It is at that time at its furthest north and blows from ENE to NE, strength about 4 on the Beaufort scale." It is astonishing how many errors get into print! If I do not sight land tomorrow or the day after at the very latest, nothing will make sense and I shall give up. When I left, on longitude about 15° 20', I took my sight at about 1210 hours; today I took it at 1510 hours, a difference of three hours, which must place me at 60° 20' west. Désirade is on 61°, that is to say 38 miles further west. Dominica and Marie Galante are respectively 61° 20' and 61° 12' west, that is to say 56 miles and 49 miles. Even at thirty miles a day that cannot be more than two days' sailing. If I see nothing the day after tomorrow I shall resign. I have had enough, all I can think of is poor Ginette, who must be dying a thousand deaths.

'1630 hours. Everything is stacked up against me; the wind has freshened, but is driving me to the south. My luck is right out. However, everything is not lost. Even to the south, I have a certain amount of margin, as far as Grenada, 240 miles away; but this drift is going to mean further delay.

'Everything points to land being near, except for an actual sight of it; I keep passing pieces of floating wood, and for a while I was followed by what looked like a shoal of mullet, neither of which is a normal sight on the high seas. But all I want to see is some sort of coastline!

'*Monday, 8th December*. Still nothing in sight and the wind has fallen again. I can hardly believe that people like the author of this Castaways' Handbook could be asked to write something for the official use of the American Navy and fill it with nothing but mis-statements. It says that a frigate bird has never been seen more than three hundred miles from the coast. Only admitting the evidence of the last one I saw, five days ago, there cannot have been more than three hundred miles to go even then.

'Saturday morning I again saw three tropic birds together. That is even more precise evidence: three of them means that land is sixty or eighty miles away, say a hundred miles to be fair, and if I made forty miles from Saturday to Sunday and another forty since, there can only be another twenty to go. Still nothing in sight and another broiling day in prospect. I have been at sea fifty days, which would mean that I have made an average of only fifty-four miles a day, although at the start I managed much more, and must have averaged thirty miles a day since, except for one day. The wind has died right down again.

'I took eleven days for the 555-mile lap to the Canaries. This passage is five times as long, and should have taken me fifty-five days, which means, I suppose, that I shall arrive on Saturday.

'There is very little fresh water left, and I cannot face the idea of sea-water with this bad diarrhoea; am catching very few fish; they must be getting suspicious. This does not really matter as there are plenty of flying fish. If things come to the worst, I always have my reserve stock of emergency food, but once I have eaten that it would be all over. Whoever writes a book for castaways based on my experiences will have to give entirely different figures for the distance from land indicated by the birds. This one must be hundreds of miles out. Feeling very disheartened, but somehow I must find the strength to carry on. If only I knew my exact longitude! If I was absolutely sure of my position, however far there was to go, I would feel a bit better. The ship and plane routes must lie to the west of the islands, in the Caribbean, which is why there are none to be seen. And to think that in strong winds I have had the sea anchor out for whole days, while now my sail is drooping uselessly! God, what can I do to end this terrible uncertainty?

'The day is going to be unbearably hot, without a cloud to mask the sun. Luck seems dead against me. I can see it raining on the horizon but not a drop comes anywhere near; there are clouds all round, but I get nothing but burning sun. This is supposed to be the regular trade wind season, but I seem to get one day of wind, one with a breeze and then two or three of flat calm. The dinghy is practically stationary. I can still see my green fluorescent patch after three days, it must be moving with the current too. And it has been this way since Saturday, 22nd; that makes twenty days of near immobility. I am not likely to forget them, I must have been crazy to put any confidence in a book written by specialists. Unfortunately it looks as if I am not going to live to put their facts right for them. Twenty days of calm when "the trade wind is at its strongest and most regular"! With this weather I cannot possibly get there alive, and yet there cannot be all that way to go. I keep seeing bits of tree bark and pieces of cork, but my sail is still flapping. Thirty or fifteen hundred miles to go, it is all the same.

'1430 hours. This is another day like last Friday; flat calm and a flapping sail. Hurrah for the trade wind! Perhaps this is one of the signs that I am near land, in which case just let me catch sight of it. Outlook for to-morrow: the same. I am not moving an inch. It is now forty-eight hours since I saw my famous group of birds, yet I estimate I must have covered eighty miles.

'1600 hours. I must say, I would like a swim and a look at the bottom of the boat. At least the dinghy will arrive intact, even if this goes on another month, unless we meet a swordfish.

'1630 hours. The sea is rising slightly, proof that there must be wind somewhere, but I am hardly getting a puff. Am hot and thirsty. Please God I live long enough to drink two quarts of milk at one gulp. Think of all the baths I have taken in my life without drinking a drop of the water. What a topsy-turvy world! At home it does not matter whether I turn off the tap or not; here a couple of gallons means the difference between life and death.

'1700 hours. Whether I am forty miles from Dominica or not I shall never get there because there is no wind. [And then, in a jumbled handwriting which I cannot recognize as my own, I noted]: another awful day!

'Have run again through my calculations of position:

'19th October, at 15° west, took position at 1215 hours;

'14th November, took position at 1400 hours, a difference of one hour forty-five minutes, which gives 41° west. This means that by then I had covered 1,568 miles, at an average of fifty-nine miles a day;

'8th December, sun at zenith at 1510 hours, that makes it 59° west, or a run of 1,044 miles since the 14th, at an average of forty-three and a half miles a day. That leaves only another 116 miles, so those birds must have been two or three hundred miles out to sea. According to the chart, I should sight something Wednesday or Thursday, at worst Friday, provided I get a little wind, although there is not much sign of it.'

It was during this period of uneventful calm that I had the most dangerous encounter of all. Sitting in the stern of L'Hérétique, watching the feeble wake, I saw appear, still some way off, a flat, black undulating mass in the water. As it came nearer, I saw it had white patches which caught the sun. When it was about fifty feet away I realized that it was a giant ray. Contrary to all logic I somehow felt reassured and took out the cine-camera to film it, without stopping to think that it probably regarded me as a good meal. It followed me for about two hours, keeping its distance all the time. Then it suddenly disappeared as if sucked down to the depths. It was only after my return that a fisherman from Dakar told me: 'That was probably your moment of greatest danger; the ray could have capsized you with a single flip of a fin or could have leapt clean out of the water on top of you.'

'*Tuesday*, 9th December, 1500 hours. A slight wind since seven o'clock yesterday evening; if only it holds! Sun as hot as ever today; had nightmares all night; still nothing in sight, hardly to be wondered at at this rate of progress. Saw three more tropic birds this morning, calling to each other, and they say that birds make no noise when they are far out to sea. Have drawn up the menu for the dinner I am going to have at the expense of one of my acquaintances, who bet me that I would never make it. In fact, I have devised three alternatives: Either *foie gras truffé, soufflé aux crevettes, canard au sang, pommes paille, fromages variés, omelette flambée à la confiture,* and *fruits rafraîchis au champagne;* or else, *homard Thermidor, perdreau truffé sur canapé, haricots verts, fromages variés, crêpe Suzette* (a dozen), *fruits rafraîchis au champagne;* or, even better, *bouquet d'écrevisses,* a dozen *escargots, lièvre à la royale, pommes vapeur* or *cuissot de chevreuil, fromages variés, omelette flambée aux confitures, ananas au kirsch à la crème.* For wine: Muscadet, Pommard '28, Vosne-Romanée 1930, Mounton-Rothschild 1947, Château-Yquem 1929, Vielle Cure and a cigar.'

CHAPTER XIV

'ARAKAKA' AND ARRIVAL

∽ ∽ ∽ ∽ ∽ ∽ ∽ ∽ ∽ ∽ ∽ ∽ ∽ ∽

THE next day the miracle happened . . . and it was another Wednesday. By then it required an effort to get up in the morning; I usually woke about sun-up, but I was in no hurry to look round the horizon, having become convinced that it would be as empty as ever. I usually continued to lie in my sleeping bag until the rays of the sun, rising in the sky, started to get hot. That morning, at about ten o'clock, I took a cursory glance outside the tent and then jumped as if I had been given an electric shock. 'A ship,' I shouted almost involuntarily. And there on the starboard quarter, about two and a half miles away, was a ship on a course which must bring it across my own. It was a big cargo boat of about seven thousand tons, making quite slow speed. There was no sign that I had been sighted and I fumbled feverishly for my heliograph to flash the sun's rays into the eyes of those on the bridge, like a child trying to annoy passers-by. At the end of what seemed an interminable wait someone saw me, and the ship changed course to cut across my stern.

My morale had risen at one bound. I was convinced that the ship must be just short of its destination in one of the West Indies harbours. I had been right all the time, I was near land. I waved my little tricolor flag on the end of an oar. Imagine how proud I was when the ship, as it drew near, ran up a Union Jack to the peak and then dipped it three times: the salute given to warships met on the high seas. I replied by waving my own little flag. When we were abeam, the captain switched on his loud hailer and asked: 'Do you need any assistance?'

'Just the time, please, and my exact longitude,' I replied.

'49° 50'.'

I was exactly ten degrees, that is to say six hundred miles, from my estimated position. I felt as if someone had hit me over the head with a hammer. It was more than I could stand. Seizing the scull, I made for the boat, muttering feverishly to myself: 'This is it, fifty-three days, I give up.' The captain hailed me again: 'Will you come aboard?'

'I will get the dinghy hoisted in, the experiment is over,' I thought. 'After all, fifty-three days must prove something.'

I bumped the ship's side and climbed on board. She was the *Arakaka*, a big passenger cargo steamer out of Liverpool. I was met by a short, sturdy man, about fifty years old, who was in a state of considerable excitement, Captain Carter of Liverpool. He asked me straight away: 'Would you like us to take you and your equipment on board? We are making for Georgetown, British Guiana.'

My first reaction was to answer yes, but then I remembered my experience with the *Sidi Ferruch*. I thought of my friends, and the seafaring folk at Boulogne who would say: 'So you didn't get across the Atlantic after all.'

The fifty-three days the voyage had lasted would have served no purpose. Although I had sufficiently proved my theory, the man in the street, or rather the ordinary seaman, would regard my giving up at this point as invalidating the whole experiment. If I was to be instrumental in saving all those human lives, then my success had to be complete. Only thus could I render a real

service to the world of the sea. I pulled myself together
and asked the captain for a few minutes to make up my
mind. In the meantime he offered me a freshwater
shower, which I accepted with gratitude. While I let the
delicious water run over me I heard one officer remark to
another in the passage:

'You have to hand it to the French, they will try
anything.'

That made my mind up. I would go on. I made a quick
mental calculation and realized that at my present speed
I would need another twenty days to reach land. It was
then 10th December, which meant arriving about 3rd
January. In order to take my position with certainty I was
going to need the Pilot Book for 1953.

The captain came to see me again while I was in the
shower and said: 'Wouldn't you like a meal?'

I declined vigorously, but he insisted:

'You can't refuse a hot meal.'

It was my first proper meal in fifty-three days and I
remember it well. There was a fried egg, a little piece of
liver, a spoonful of cabbage and some fruit. Not only was
I to be reproached later for eating it, but it gave me the
worst stomach trouble of the whole voyage. I sent off
a telegram to my wife and was shown round the ship.
I shall always remember the luxurious officers' ward-
room, with its leather arm-chairs. The table was laid for
lunch. The passengers lived in true British comfort.
Noting all this, I repeated to myself: 'Another twenty
days, another twenty days.' The captain took me into the
charthouse, showed me my exact position and gave me
a note of the declinations I would have to observe as I
approached the land. He gave me a Pilot Book with the
1953 figures, and presented me with a copy of the superb
British Admiralty Sailing Instructions, which he dedi-
cated to me.

Then, crossing the deck with slightly uncertain steps, but still perfectly firm on my feet, I made for the rail, where they had put down a Jacob's ladder for me to regain L'Hérétique. Most of the crew were there to cheer me on, promising to meet again on land, and the captain seemed much moved. Just as I was about to go down the ladder he cried: 'What can I do for you, you must let me do something. Is there nothing that would be of assistance?'

Then I remembered that I had heard no Bach during the whole of the journey and said that I would very much like to hear on Christmas night the Sixth Brandenburg Concerto. (One of the gifts I had received on board the *Arakaka* was a new battery for my wireless set.)

'I'll turn the world upside down if necessary,' he replied. 'I give you my word, you will have your Concerto for Christmas.'

I dropped the tow-line, and the *Arakaka* waited for me to stand off a little before starting her engines, so that my fragile craft should not be sucked into the powerful propellers. A light breeze had sprung up and I was in a hurry to take advantage of it, so I hoisted my sail and set course for the west. Our meeting had lasted an hour and a half. The *Arakaka* slowly gathered way and, amidst the bellowing of her siren, dipped her flag three times again in salute.

I knew that I was going to regret the *Arakaka* and that sometimes I was going to think: 'Why did I not take advantage of the captain's offer, it was probably my last chance?' But for my experiment to be a success, it was absolutely essential for me to continue, to press on, and in the end it was the decision of which I was most proud. The entry in my log-book that day read:

'*Wednesday*, 10th *December*. Wednesday must be my lucky day, I have just been on board a ship, have had a light meal, and am on my way again. Alas, I am only on the fiftieth meridian and have another six hundred miles to go. At this speed I shall need another fifteen or twenty days. Morale high, but I still have it in for the specialists. Now at least I know how to take my longitude; cannot think how I timed my first sight at 1215 hours, it must have been at least 1300, and the noon sun will now give me my true position. Ginette has had a message and the voyage continues. God is good. It was the cargo steamer *Arakaka*, Captain Carter, out of Liverpool, destination Guiana. I have to admit I very nearly stayed on board.'

Only the merest chance could have arranged such a meeting in that part of the ocean, and I might quite easily have continued on my voyage without seeing a thing. In that case it is more than likely that I would have gone mad. Convinced of my proximity to land, I had been spending more and more of my time scanning the horizon, tiring my eyes, wearing myself out and becoming a little more demoralized each day. The blessed *Arakaka* not only saved me by reassuring my family, but raised my morale. At last I knew where I was and could determine my longitude with precision. The captain had pointed out to me in the Pilot Book a little table, called the time equation, which supplied a small correction to subtract from the hour the sun reached its zenith. As long as I could determine this time, I could not be more than sixty miles out in my calculations. I could now navigate with confidence: my watch had been put right and the new radio battery I had been so kindly given enabled me to make a further check.

That day and for some days following I had no appetite for fish; unfortunately that was all there was to eat; the snack I had eaten on board *Arakaka* was having its effect. In due course, back in Paris again, a famous expert on nutrition told me: 'If we had known you had a meal on

H

the ship you met, we would not have rated your chances of survival very high.' What now happened to me was identical with the experience of political deportees and liberated prisoners of war. I had taken two forms of nourishment. Before my little meal on the fifty-third day, my food had been abnormal. Afterwards, losing all appetite for fish, I became undernourished. The human organism gradually accustoms itself to a change and diminution in the normal ration, but after a proper meal, the digestive system seems to say: 'There, things are back to normal again, I need to make no further special effort,' rather like an athlete who stops in the middle of a race and finds he cannot start again. The stomach becomes prey to a sort of despair. I lost more weight (the photographs prove it) during the twelve days still remaining to land than in the fifty-three days prior to my meeting with the *Arakaka*.

I had now made up my mind on the value to be attached to books written for the benefit of castaways, with all their hints on navigation, signs that land is near and all the evidence of floating timber, butterflies, gossamer threads, flies and birds. Do not take it too hard, dear author of the Raft Book; whether the frigate bird can spend a night at sea or not I do not know, but it is certainly to be found fifteen hundred miles from land. It is also incorrect to say that it does not catch its own fish, as I have seen them swoop on the flying fish chased out of the sea by the dolphins.

How had I managed to make such hopeless miscalculations of my position? I took my first sight on leaving the Canaries in a very rough sea and must have mistaken the crest of a wave for the horizon. By a curious combination of error, I had obtained my correct latitude, but was an hour out in the time. I thought I had determined the 15° of longitude at 1215, when in reality it

was one o'clock in the afternoon. I had therefore con-
cluded that I must make a correction of forty-five minutes,
that is to say a minimum of 10°. When I thought I had
reached 60° west, I was only at 50° west, and still had
another six hundred miles to go.

I wanted to reach French territory, particularly as they
were the only West Indian islands with a protected
harbour on the east coast. I therefore tried to keep on the
latitude of Martinique, always prepared to drift towards
Barbados if the north wind persisted. I ran the risk,
nevertheless, of being carried to the south of the British
island and seeing my route prolonged by some three
hundred miles. Three days after meeting the *Arakaka*, I
encountered the most curious weather of the whole
voyage. As soon as the morning had passed, a flat calm
descended again, but an endless stream of little, woolly
clouds, quite low, hurried past right above me. The
dinghy barely moved and the whole day I sat there in an
impotent rage, watching the clouds scudding towards
land.

Fortunately I did not spend the day alone. A somewhat
embarrassing companion, but at least a companion, put
in an appearance. A thunderous snort suddenly attracted
my attention off to the left and I saw coming towards me
a large whale. I feared at first that the beast would come
too near the dinghy and damage it with its flukes, but
although it had several good looks, it never came nearer
than a dozen feet or so. It moved ponderously round the
boat most of the day and then, at dusk, gravely made off,
never to be seen again.

In the meantime a storm was gathering. At about one
o'clock in the morning the first big waves started to toss
my cockle-shell around. The final days were not going
to spare me. During the twenty days of storm I had
already endured, I had been swamped twice, but I had

to put up with four more involuntary duckings during the twelve days that remained. Fortunately I had perfected my baling procedure. Once the dinghy was full of water, I started to empty it with my linen hat, five or six pints at a time, getting down to the fine work later with a shoe. The simplest methods are often the best when dealing with the elements.

My chief joy was to see the sail filled again to bursting and to hear once more the characteristic hiss of my best speed – about three knots. In the absence of a log, the noise the dinghy made through the water enabled me to estimate my speed.

The more progress I made, the greater was my fear that some stupid accident would ruin everything just as I was within sight of success. There was still the dread that one wave might be more destructive than the others, nullifying at one blow my successful survival of all previous dangers. In a duel with the sea, not a moment's relaxation is permitted, but I still remember my shouts of joy as I felt the wind whistling in my ears.

I finally settled down to sleep quite happily, but was woken abruptly with the feeling that something unusual was going on. I got up. The sea aft was criss-crossed by the phosphorescent wake of some huge fish. I never discovered whether it was a swordfish or a shark, but it had invented a new and dangerous game. Swimming straight at the raft, it ducked underneath it just at the last moment, rasping the bottom with its back. This went on for six hours. Exasperated, I finally made up my mind to attack it, whereupon the beast disappeared as rapidly as it had arrived. The next morning, although no wave had hit L'Hérétique during the night, I found that I was wet through. It was only too clear that the boat was beginning to leak and that my nocturnal visitor must have damaged the fabric sufficiently with his sandpaper back to reduce its impermeability. It was high time I reached my destination; my situation was becoming distinctly uncomfortable. The floats seemed to have come through unscathed and kept up their air pressure, but as water was seeping slowly through the whole of the bottom of the boat it was impossible to repair the leak. A proper hole would have been easy. Every five hours or so, when the water reached the deck boards, I had to bale, and this went on during the whole ten days that remained before I touched land.

The birds became more and more numerous and varied. At last, on 13th December, the first seagull appeared, and I was back in familiar territory. During the day I was able to film a fantastic scene. For some days a frigate bird, surely one of the most handsome sea-birds in existence, had been keeping me company and dived from time to time to catch a flying fish. I had been puzzled to understand exactly how this bird knew how to be at the exact spot when its prey took flight. I suddenly realized that it was working in collaboration with the dolphins. These used to make a sudden concerted assault on a shoal of flying fish, scattering them into the air, and then chasing them, often leaping out of the water themselves in the process. As soon as the bird saw the hunt begin, it dived towards the pack and came up every time with a flying fish in its beak. Rising to a considerable height, it would drop the fish suddenly, diving rapidly underneath its line of fall to catch it head first in its wide-open beak. A quick gulp and it was gone, an almost perfect example of refuelling in mid-air. The most extraordinary thing was to see the fish planing along in parallel flight with the bird. Camera in hand I tried to record this astonishing sight.

The light meal I had eaten on board the *Arakaka* had the most curious effects. First of all my attack of diarrhoea died down overnight, although I half expected the contrary, as cabbage and fruit have a laxative effect. Another result was no less surprising and rather more unpleasant. The meal had restored my normal appetite. It was not until after I had eaten it on 10th December that I began to feel hungry. I suffered thereafter from terrible stomach cramps, although my food supplies were the same and as plentiful as before meeting the ship. I started to yawn like a starving man, something which had never happened in the fifty preceding days. I had nightmares about food every time I went to sleep, with one image appearing like a *leitmotiv*: a dish of chicken with rice. I still cannot understand why.

I spent the whole of 20th December remembering all the good meals I had eaten since the war, particularly during the weeks which led up to my departure. Having calculated that, barring accidents, I had about as many more days at sea as my stay at Casablanca had lasted, I tried to remember with each meal of plankton and fish the menu I had eaten on land for each corresponding day: 'Today', I was able to say, 'I lunched at Admiralty House on *lièvre à la royale*; this evening with the Casablanca Medical Association on *rognons au vin blanc*.'

        o   *o*   *o*   *o*   *o*   *o*   *o*   *o*   *o*

I had at last changed my chart. I had finished with the general chart of the Atlantic and was now marking my position on that of the approaches to the Caribbean. The only drawback was that its larger scale gave me the impression that I had further to go. To mark this event I threw into the sea my last message in a bottle. It read: 'Experiment successful, mission practically accomplished.

Will finder please forward this message to . . .' I wanted
to see whether any of these messages had been picked up.

I considered myself as good as there. The day of the
21st ended with the appearance in my wake of a fish
about five feet long, with a pointed snout and an impressive set of teeth. It was the first barracuda I caught. He
seemed to look at me with a hungry air. I was afraid of
him at first and threw my little winch at him on the end
of a line, the method I usually used to scare off sharks,
which normally made off at top speed. This beast was in
no way put out and continued to follow me with a
menacing air. I then fixed my bent knife to the end of the
underwater gun and after wounding him two or three
times sunk the blade deep into his body. I thus put an end
to this particular argument and although I give the
creature full marks for courage, I did not appreciate his
indigestible flesh. Then, on the 22nd, when I woke up
just before sunrise, imagine my surprise to see that I had
just been passed by a large cargo boat. I was just in its
wake and it seemed impossible that I should not have
been sighted. Determined to send off more news, I let
off a flare to make the ship turn round and find out why
it had ignored me.

But the vessel continued slowly on its way and I
thought for a moment that it had not even seen the flare.
Seizing my last one, I threw it in the air, where it formed
a bright, luminous trail. This time the ship turned round
and came back until I was almost alongside. She was by
no means as easy to board as the *Arakaka* because the sea
was much rougher, but once on deck I found out that
she was a Dutch cargo ship bound for Port of Spain in
Trinidad, the most southerly of the West Indies. I had
made up my mind to ask them to advise Martinique and
Barbados of my imminent arrival and to see if they would
give me something to eat – not fish – to enable me to

spend Christmas in a dignified fashion if I should still be at sea. The captain received me in a very friendly fashion and offered me a cup of coffee. My position was confirmed; I was, as I had calculated, at 13° 50′ north, 58° 20′ west. Then the conversation took an extraordinary turn:

'Captain,' I said, 'how did you manage to pass so close without seeing me?'

'But we did see you,' he replied. 'We passed quite close, circled right round you, and not seeing any sign of life we assumed that it was an abandoned dinghy and continued on our way. It was only your signals that brought us back.'

'No sign of life, sir?' I retorted. 'My sail was set, the rudder fixed, my wireless aerial was up, how can you call that no sign of life? Moreover, you recognized me as soon as I was introduced to you. Supposing I had been a real castaway, half dead and incapable of making any signal, would you have abandoned me to my fate?'

As far as I could make out the captain had simply not thought of this and, incredible as it may seem, it had not even occurred to him to sound his siren to see if that brought any signs of life.

The reader should not suppose that this was an exceptional case. We had already noticed in the Mediterranean, that passenger liners seemed to consider that the necessity of adhering to a strict time schedule took precedence over rescue work. They are no longer ships, but trains running on the sea. Unless a passenger drew the captain's attention to something unusual, the 'train' just rolled on.

I clambered down again into the dinghy and, after marking my position on the chart, realized that the end was in sight. I had another seventy miles to cover, on a course of two hundred and thirty-two; that is to say, to the south-west, to reach the north coast of Barbados. The wind was strong and, after making a rough calculation of my speed, I expected to see the lighthouse on the northern point (a white light with a double flash, at an interval of ten seconds, visible twenty miles) between midnight and two in the morning.

It was a tiring day, as although I realized that it was highly unlikely I should see anything, I scanned the horizon ceaselessly in the hope of a miraculous early arrival. I slept quite well during the early part of the evening and then woke up for my last watch. At half past midnight, the sky was suddenly illuminated by a bright flash, followed almost immediately by a second. Grabbing my watch, I timed the next pair of flashes: they were exactly ten seconds apart. For the first time in sixty-five days I had regained contact with land; the flashes were the reflection of the lighthouse beam on the clouds. I must have been about sixteen miles from the northern point of Barbados and therefore had another dozen hours before having to contend with the problem of landing. I could perfectly well have gone to sleep again, but nearly hysterical with excitement at the proximity of land – I had almost ceased to believe in its very existence – I sat transfixed on one of the floats, watching the regular flashes, counting again and again the time interval between them, each pair seeming a new miracle, and indeed for me they were. It took me nearly two hours to convince myself that I was not dreaming.

Barbados is one of the most difficult West Indian islands to approach from the eastern side, unless you have a minute knowledge of the coast. The northern part consists entirely of rocky cliffs, against which the waves thunder incessantly, and to the south there is a barrier of reefs about a mile out to sea. Although there are a number of passages through into the lagoon, no one without

*H

intimate knowledge would dare to risk them. During the eighteenth century it was on this section of the coast that the notorious Sam Lord lured ships to their destruction. He planted two parallel rows of coconut palms, on which he fixed red and white lights to look like the entrance to a harbour. Ships used to hurl themselves on the reefs and Sam Lord sent his black slaves to massacre the entire crew so that no witnesses should survive. Any slave returning without at least one head was immediately put to death, thus ensuring that they gave no quarter. The cargo was then salvaged, and Lord became a fabulously wealthy man.

Sam Lord had been dead for two hundred years, but it was still impossible for me to land on that part of the coast, and I had two alternatives: either to make for a stretch of about four miles on the northern part of the coast, where landing was just possible, or to round the point, throw out my sea anchor in the deep water to the west and try to attract the attention of the harbour authorities at Speightstown. At daybreak I was surprised to see that I was much nearer the island than I thought, only four or five miles off. My emotions were very different from those at the time of my landing on the Canaries, but my chances of rounding the northern point and avoiding the mortal dangers of the eastern coast were as problematical as they had been on the earlier occasion.

For the first time during the whole Atlantic passage, I let down my lee-boards to take the wind abeam, in an attempt to round the foaming northern cliff. Admiral Sol had warned me to take the greatest possible precautions while attempting to beach the dinghy. Perhaps my experience will be of some assistance to future castaways. If I can offer a word of advice, it is this: once in sight of land, the worst seems over, but remember the danger of being killed by the very land which promises salvation.

Take your time. Impatience can ruin everything. Stop the boat, observe the coast closely and choose your point. Never forget that ninety per cent of all accidents occur on landing. You must choose a stretch where the sea beats less violently, where there is sand or beach and not some murderous rock. The way to determine this is by observing the colour and nature of the sea; little white caps probably hide a reef, so take care. Make only for smooth stretches without turbulence or breaking waves.

I managed to round the point, and then started winking my heliograph at all the farms and sugar factories lining the coast. Along this stretch, the sea was no longer disordered but roared ashore in long impressive lines of surf. I had covered about half a mile, when I had a terrible shock: almost on the beach a boat containing five men appeared to be in difficulties. Had they seen me, and was this an attempt to beat through the surf to my assistance? Caught in a wave, the boat disappeared, and when I saw it again the five men were no longer in it. I was terribly agitated. Had these men thought I was in difficulties and, in coming out to my assistance, lost two or three lives? I stood in for the shore as fast as I could. When we were within hailing distance I realized with surprise that they were negroes who had not even seen me. They were fishermen and had to risk their lives in this sea as a matter of course every day. Sea urchins are their principal catch, and as the boat tosses over the clear water, one of the crew dives in, however high the waves, prepared to be carried with his catch two hundred yards to the sandy shore. I was by this time three hundred yards out, and had made up my mind that this was the point to land; it took me three more hours to get there. Now I had found a stretch of sand, my life was no longer in danger. The dinghy was undamaged and all its equipment intact, but I took special care to protect my precious log notes, with all the details I hoped would help to save the lives of so many future castaways.

The final manœuvre was exhausting for anybody as worn out as I was. As on most of the African and Caribbean surf beaches, the waves did not break with equal force, but with a clearly defined rhythm which differs from place to place. The seventh and the sixteenth are usually the most dangerous and must be met with extreme care. At this point, every seventh wave seemed the strongest. The wind was abeam and I turned the dinghy to present the stern to the shore. At the third wave in each series I turned about to gain some distance towards the shore. After the fifth I faced out to sea again to take the force of the seventh wave by the bow. Laboriously, I covered a few yards at a time, but each successive seventh wave became more and more dangerous. The fishermen who had seen me did not yet seem to realize that there was anything unusual in my arrival or that any boat coming from my direction must hail from the far off lands of their ancestors. Soon I was surrounded by three boats, and entered into a shouted conversation in highly inventive English with their occupants. Then three of the negroes plunged in and climbed on board L'Hérétique; for the first time in my Atlantic passage I had a crew. They were something of a pest, ferreting everywhere, examining everything and rocking the boat from one side to the other. One of them asked me for my watch, but when he found that its tick was hardly to be heard, handed it back with a disdainful air. Another seemed fascinated by a piece of soap which he apparently wanted to eat. The third pounced on my binoculars, which he put to his eyes the wrong way round, and then solemnly scanned the horizon. When I explained to him that they were full of water and useless, he started to shake them as if to empty a bottle.

Although I was as good as there, I began to worry about my log-books and the emergency store of food, which I intended to deposit intact at the first police station. But I was too worn out to keep an eye on everything. I therefore made up my mind to find two or three reliable witnesses as soon as I could, who would confirm that I had not touched my provisions.

L'Hérétique was still about twenty yards from the beach, which soon changed in colour from yellow to black as the local inhabitants gathered. The fishermen tried to persuade me to wait for the ebb tide before landing, saying that the waves would be less strong. What they really wanted was time to search the whole dinghy before those on shore had a chance. But the desire to touch land, to smell it, to know the feel of warm sand was too strong. Knowing that the dinghy would survive the breaking waves, and exasperated by the uselessness of my new crew, I dived in, swam the remaining twenty yards with L'Hérétique's anchor and, aided by scores of people, hauled her ashore. The beach seemed to pitch and toss under my feet, but I was so transported with delight that the hunger pains from which I had been suffering disappeared in a flash.

If I may give a last word of advice to future castaways, it is to avoid at all cost too quick or too large a meal on arrival. It would probably kill you. Take all the liquid you like, but go carefully with the solids, sworn enemies of a weakened digestion. Having snatched your life from the sea, do not let the land take it from you. A long bout with hunger can become, once safe, a fight against the greater menace of a surfeit of food.

CHAPTER XV

LANDFALL

◇ ◇ ◇ ◇ ◇ ◇ ◇ ◇ ◇ ◇ ◇

ALTHOUGH the Barbados beach seemed to rock and shift under my feet, it felt to me like the Promised Land. To this day I do not know how I found the strength to walk across it, but walk I did. I had to keep a sharp eye on my equipment, as the people gathered on the beach seemed to regard the contents of the boat as some sort of manna from heaven, seizing everything within their grasp. In a flash, they emptied the box of cigarettes which Captain Carter's wife had given me on board the *Arakaka*. One of them picked up my underwater harpoon gun, for which there were no harpoons left, and after asking what it was used for seemed extremely flattered when I made him a present of it. Someone else made off with an old shirt, and a third made signs that he had taken a fancy to the watch on my wrist. When I told him it was the only one I had, he pointed to my wrist compass and said, 'But there you have another one.'

In spite of these hindrances, I managed to unload the dinghy little by little, making a separate pile of anything that had been damaged, including a number of things which had suffered at the last moment when the dinghy became completely waterlogged under the battering of the final waves. Then, with the help of a few spectators, I pulled out the still sealed crate of food. When they saw on it the word 'rations' they shouted, 'Food! Food!'

I saw that it was going to be impossible for me to keep an eye on everything. At any moment I might find the food crate broken open, which, even if I had salvaged the contents, would have destroyed the evidence for my theory. By then a local policeman had arrived with the information that the nearest station was two miles away. (I had to get there on foot, and how I made it, I cannot imagine.) I had the presence of mind to take immediate steps to prove that my food reserve was intact. One or two of the more intelligent spectators agreed to serve as witness, and I chose the local schoolmistress and lay-preacher, together with the policeman. Then I handed round my American tinned food, which was received with delight.

I have since been reproached for not immediately placing my log-books under seal, as proof that I had had no time to falsify the entries. I can only answer such arm-chair criticism by asking how much can be expected from someone who has just reached land after sixty-five days of total isolation and immobility. Slowly, pushed and pulled by the natives, drinking a glass of water at every turning, bathed in sweat and exhausted, I finally reached the police station. The officer in charge was clearly at a loss to decide whether I was a pirate or an exceptionally foolhardy yachtsman, but with the splendid correctitude of the British policeman, who is at the same time father-confessor to those confided to his charge, he sat me down in front of a cup of tea and a piece of bread and butter. I had begun the battle involved in returning to a normal diet; I therefore restricted myself to the tea with several spoonfuls of sugar. The scene was certainly picturesque, with the police station surrounded by hundreds of people all dressed in the bright colours so dear to the inhabitants of these islands.

Finally, at about eleven o'clock, I received a personal

telephone call from Colonel Reggie Michelin, Commissioner of Police in Barbados (now Commissioner in Jamaica). This seemed to make a favourable impression on the local officer, who offered me a shower.

The Commissioner had told me that a car was on its way to take me to Bridgetown, and I arrived in the capital at about two o'clock in the afternoon. My first question was to ask whether the yacht *Nymph Errant* had arrived.

'It got here on 1st December, twenty-three days ago,' I was told, 'but I think it has left again for Antigua to await the arrival of Ann Davison.'

It looked as though there had been a slight misunderstanding with the captain of the *Arakaka*, because when he asked me where I expected to land I had said the Antilles. Now the British phrase for the Antilles is the West Indies, and he must have understood Antigua, and had sent off a message to that place. I presumed that my friends the Stanilands had gone there in the hope of meeting both Ann Davison and me. Someone else, however, reported that the yacht was still in the basin.

I was received by the colonel, a typical Briton, young and dynamic, who had with him the French Consul, Mr Collins. After explaining in broad terms that I hoped to rest up for a few days before returning to France, I saw another car arrive. In it were my three friends, John, Bonnie and Winnie, who shouted with joy at the sight of me and insisted that I was to regard their yacht as my home. I accepted with delight, and resigned myself to staying rather longer than I expected. They were accompanied by one of the local physicians, Dr David Payne, who shortly afterwards gave me a very thorough physical examination in order to determine the exact consequences of my ordeal. I was still feeling quite sprightly, fairly steady on my legs and even capable of walking around and climbing a few stairs. It was only during the days

that followed that I started to pay the price for the
immobility, protracted solitude and abnormal life I had
just experienced.

I complied with the Customs formalities, sent messages
off to France through the charming Consul and by six
o'clock was on board the *Nymph Errant*. Although I had
decided to take nothing but liquid nourishment for at
least a week, I now gave up the idea and began to eat a
little solid food. I retired to my cabin in a state of nervous
exhaustion, but found it impossible to sleep. I started
tinkering with my radio, taking off the nylon cover
which had protected it and cleaning the parts so that I
could take it back to France in the best possible
condition.

At about ten o'clock I tuned it in to the BBC, and to
the stupefaction of my friends we heard the announcer
of the BBC Overseas Service say in French:

'Doctor Bombard, we have received the message from
the captain of the *Arakaka*; and wish to express our
appreciation of your work on behalf of castaways and
the hope that this message reaches you somewhere at sea
in L'Hérétique. We shall be playing for you tomorrow the
Brandenburg Concerto at such-and-such a time on such-
and-such a wavelength. (I do not remember the details
now.) Please have your set tuned in.'

The next day, by then advised of my arrival in Barbados, the BBC sent me a telegram to confirm that they
would play the Concerto just the same. During the day
the two things happened which could afford me the
greatest pleasure, apart from the message I received from
my wife: the Royal Barbados Yacht Club announced that
I had been elected an honorary member for the duration
of my stay in the island, and I received a cable from
Captain Carter:

'Congratulations to a gallant gentleman who had so

much courage in his convictions to carry on when safety and luxury were proposed. Signed: Carter.'

This message has always been a consolation during the attacks to which I was subsequently subjected. The man I had met in the middle of the ocean, a true seaman, had sent me a token of his esteem, admiration and friendship.

I spent a week of complete enchantment in Barbados, in spite of the cumulative effects of exhaustion, which obliged me first to carry a stick and then to give up walking almost completely. I was driven all round this island paradise, accustoming myself again to the hues of green which the blue of the sea and sky had almost made me forget, a rich verdant green, as Christmas-time is the Caribbean spring.

I was most hospitably received by the Governor who, as a former prisoner of the Japanese, was able to appreciate better than anyone the moral effect of my recent experiences. A flood of congratulatory telegrams arrived from France, and the people in the streets, with their friendly familiarity greeted me at each turn with, 'Hullo, Doc'.

All this was most reassuring and comforting. With my beard I became almost a legendary figure in Bridgetown, and the French colony there made me their honoured guest. However, it was time for me to leave the enchanted isles and return to France where Ginette, as she had said in her telegram, and my friends were awaiting me impatiently.

On 31st December the British West Indies Airways Company flew me as far as Puerto Rico. Calling on the way at Antigua, I learnt to my delight that Ann Davison, who had left the Canaries some time after I did, had got as far as the island of Dominica. I immediately sent off a message to my friends the Stanilands with the news, which I knew would reassure them on her account.

Arriving at Puerto Rico, I was passing through the immigration authorities when, to my astonishment, the American inspector threw up his hands in horror because I had no visa. It was useless for me to insist that I was only in transit. The Immigration Law had been altered while I was at sea, and I needed a transit visa to pass through the United States. I was unable to continue my journey and had to stay where I was.

The crew of the British plane which had brought me thus far saw to it that I was installed in a luxurious hotel in the town to wait for the visa, which they assured me could not take long. Without it I would have to return through the British West Indies to Forte de France and leave there for home direct. It was no easy matter to get a visa on New Year's Day as everyone was on holiday. The immigration officers were most understanding, went to great pains and after a twenty-four hours' wait in the charming town of San Juan de Puerto Rico I was authorized to continue my journey and given a visa valid for thirty days. I took off under a mild spring sun and on arrival in New York found my friend Percy Knauth waiting for me.

The city was enveloped in a snowstorm and it was terribly cold. I had not felt as frozen in a year, as most of my passage across the Atlantic had been in the tropics. Barely a week earlier I had spent Christmas night stretched out on a beach under twinkling stars in the warm night air.

The air trip had worn me out and I was obliged to put off the crossing of the Atlantic in spite of the impatience of my family at the other end. I spent most of the days stretched out on my bed in an hotel with the charming name of The White Whale at Sag Harbour, where my friends lived. Nevertheless I had to move on; my friends in France were getting impatient. I took the plane on the evening of 6th January. The route was New York–Montreal–Gander–Paris. When we landed at Montreal I was recognized by a group of young French Canadians who congratulated me on my voyage. Camera bulbs flashed all round me, to the great astonishment of an actress who was joining the plane and who asked, pointing at me:

'Who is that?'

'Doctor Bombard,' she was told.

'Doctor Bombard?'

'That's right, the chap who has just crossed the Atlantic.'

'So what?' she replied. 'I've been across the Atlantic too.'

The indignant air hostess abandoned the good lady without attempting to explain the somewhat special conditions of my crossing. During the flight there was a brief alarm. Something had gone wrong with the heating system and it became so hot in the plane that there seemed a risk of fire. With magnificent calm, the hostess gave no indication to the passengers that there was any danger. In one of the nicest compliments ever paid to my voyage she said: 'If we ever have to put down in the sea, let us hope it is today when you are there to look after us.' Perhaps after all I had accomplished something.

On arriving at Paris, she pointed out the crowd waiting for me. I felt as nervous as if I was going to take an examination. The plane stopped, the door opened and I found myself faced by a surging crowd of welcoming friends, who had come to greet my return to French soil. The wheel had come full circle.

PART FOUR
CONCLUSIONS

CHAPTER XVI

SUMMING UP

∽ ∽ ∽ ∽ ∽ ∽ ∽ ∽ ∽ ∽ ∽

THE voyage of L'Hérétique is over. Now I have to fight for the understanding of my heresies and their acceptance as orthodox doctrine for future castaways.

Any survivor of a disaster at sea should be able to reach land in as good a physical condition as I did. Mine was a perfectly normal case and my health was that of the average man. I have had three attacks of jaundice in my life and several more or less serious ailments, due to the effects of wartime undernourishment. I therefore made the crossing with no particular physical advantages. I was somewhat shrunken on arrival, it is true, but I got there. It was not a question of living well but of surviving long enough to reach land or meet a ship.

I claim to have proved that the sea itself provides sufficient food and drink to enable the battle for survival to be fought with perfect confidence.

During the sixty-five days it took me to get from the Canaries to the West Indies I enjoyed no particular good fortune and my voyage cannot be considered an exceptional case or a mere hazardous exploit. I lost fifty-five pounds in weight and suffered various minor ills. I became seriously anaemic (my red corpuscle count was five million at the start and two and a half million on arrival), and my haemoglobin level had reached the safety limit. The period following the light meal I had on board the *Arakaka* was very nearly fatal.

My blood pressure varied greatly with my state of mind. It remained more or less normal until the beginning of December and became dangerously low as my despair increased after that date. My meeting with the *Arakaka* sent it up to normal again, after which it declined slowly with my growing fatigue. It showed clearly the effect on the system of extraneous events and their capacity to cause psychological disturbances and fluctuations in the state of health.

I was racked by an attack of diarrhoea for fourteen days, from 26th November to 10th December, with sizeable haemorrhages. I nearly lost consciousness on two occasions: on 23rd November, when I had the premonition preceding the storm and on 6th December when I wrote out my will. My skin became dehydrated and I had a rash covering my whole body. I lost the nails from my toes. I developed serious defects of vision, suffered a marked loss in muscular tone and was hungry. But I got there.

For sixty-five days I lived exclusively on what I could catch from the sea. My intake of proteins and fats was sufficient. The lack of carbohydrates doubtless contributed to my loss of weight, but I had proved that the safety margin, calculated in advance in a laboratory, was a correct estimate.

As an example of the paramount importance of mental endurance over the physical, I only need to mention the psychological hunger which I suffered after meeting the *Arakaka*, which had much more serious effects on my health than the organic hunger I endured with Palmer during our period of fast in the Mediterranean. The former variety is not true hunger, it is a desire for something else, always dangerous when the something else is not available. The latter causes pain and stomach cramp during the first forty-eight hours, which then die down, to be replaced by somnolence and general weakness. In the first instance the organism is burning itself away and in the second it goes into a sort of hibernation.

The medical examination which I underwent on arrival gave no indication of any condition caused by avitaminosis. The plankton must therefore have been a sufficient source of vitamin C.

I had no rainwater for the first twenty-three days. During the whole of that period I proved conclusively that I could quench my thirst from fish and that the sea itself provides the liquid necessary to health. After leaving Monaco, I drank sea-water for fourteen days in all and fish juice for forty-three days. I had conquered the menace of thirst at sea.

I had been told that sea-water was laxative, but during the long period of our Mediterranean fast neither Palmer nor I had a single motion for eleven days. There was no sign of the predicted auto-intoxication and my mucous membranes never became dry. I shall give a full account of my medical conclusions in the thesis I am preparing and, in collaboration with the French naval authorities, I am producing a handbook for the use of castaways which will summarize and codify the results of my experiment.

I want to assert most emphatically that a life-raft can remain at sea for much longer than ten days. It can be steered sufficiently to carry a castaway to safety. L'Hérétique was a craft of this type. I have also suggested certain rules of conduct and employment which will keep shipwrecked survivors actively occupied all day, with their hopes concentrated on the supreme object: survival. Even a man in the depths of despair can find a second wind which will enable him to pull himself together and carry on.

The bottom of a life-raft should carry printed in the

fabric a map of the prevailing winds and currents in the world's oceans. Survivors of Atlantic wrecks are compelled by these winds and currents to make for America, whatever the distance. To give them hope and convince them that they will survive their ordeal, I would like to see printed on the map: 'Remember the man who did it in 1952.'

To hope is to seek better things. The survivor of a shipwreck, deprived of everything, must never lose hope. The simple and brutal problem confronting him is that of death or survival. He will need to bolster his courage with all his resources and all his faith in life to fight off despair.

I would like to add one more thought: a human life should only be risked in such an experiment as mine if some useful purpose is being served. If there are any young people who think they see a short cut to fame in setting off in a raft for America or elsewhere, I beg them to reflect or come and see me first. Led astray by false hopes, encouraged by some initial success, or misled into thinking they are on some pleasure trip, they will not realize how desperate is the fight for life until it is too late and will no longer have the time to marshal their courage. Panic will only set in more quickly for having risked their lives to no useful purpose. There will be other and better reasons for such a sacrifice.

But you, my brother castaway, if you remain firm in belief and hope, you will see, as did Robinson Crusoe on his island, how your riches will increase from day to day. And now I trust there is no further reason for you to lose hope.